Grand Salute

Stories of the World War II Generation
A Western Pennsylvania Chronicle

By Richard Robbins

Grand Salute

Photographs courtesy of the George C. Marshall Foundation, Lexington, Virginia; Jennifer Sterbutzel and Andrew T. "Dutch" Haky, who filmed General Marshall at Connellsville Airport in September 1939; the Connellsville Historical Society; Jim Burger, on behalf of his mother Lisa; the Robbins family; Stock Montage and the Harry S. Truman Presidential Library. Front flap photograph of William Robbins, the author's father, at Camp Stoneman, California, during the war years. Photograph at end of book: Connellsville Canteen volunteers.

Richard Robbins/347 Redstone Furnace Road, Uniontown, Pennsylvania 15401. E-mail inquires to grandsalutebook@gmail.com

For Barbara, Mindy, and the grandchildren
Quinton and Bailey - words cannot express

Contents

Introduction

I interviewed my first veteran of World War II in 1970 or so. I didn't think much of it then. However, as the years rolled on, I came to realize what a distinct honor it was to tell the stories of the individuals who served their country during the greatest emergency of the 20th Century. The war years years were a complex period - rich in courage and ripe with contradiction. I think now of those who didn't return - many were mere youngsters; of the thousands of bereaved mothers and fathers, wives and children; and of the families that never were. The war encapsulated the years 1941-1945, but really the conflict blankets a much longer period. George Marshall's preparation began in his boyhood, witness, as he was, to the return of soldiers from the Spanish-American War just as the 19th century was ending. The late 1940s and the 1950s are part of the fabric of World War II as well. No one can recall those years without a deep bow to the fighting years, the years of upheaval. World War II set the stage for all that followed. I was on hand in 2004 for the unveiling of the National World War II Memorial in Washington, D.C. It was very personal for me, my father having played a small part in the great conflict. I thought of the memorial as a nod to him and to members of his generation, as indeed it is. This book represents another stone cast upon those always stirring waters.

Our sons, pride of our Nation ...
Franklin D. Roosevelt, address
to the nation, June 6, 1944

*Wars are not clean and neat, and
neither is their aftermath.*
historian Thomas Childers, from
Soldier From The War Returning

A Hero For All Time

History's child

At Home in Uniontown

George Marshall was born at the family residence on the western edge of Uniontown's Main Street on the very last day of 1880, a cold and blustery December 31. The Marshall family, renting instead of owning the sprawling brick two-story at 130 West Main, consisted of father George Sr., mother Laura, sister Marie, and older brother Stuart. The first Marshall sibling, William, had died at the age of six months and was buried at the family's ancestral home in Lexington, Kentucky.

Family life appears not to have been ordinary. In part, this was due to the times. Uniontown was growing rapidly, the surrounding countryside swelling with European immigrants employed by the local coal and coking companies. Mr. Marshall, who "came north" in 1869, was himself in the coking business. A partner with Arthur Bliss of Muscle Shoals, Alabama, the two founded Bliss, Marshall and Company. At first constructing coke ovens in Dunbar, the partners later re-formed as the Percy Mining Company and later organized the Fayette Coke and Furnace Company. Among their acquisitions: one-hundred and fifty coke ovens in Oliphant Furnace, between Uniontown and Fairchance. Mr. Marshall was a fair to good businessman, and was always a hard worker; unlucky and ill-advised in some ways, he survived good times and bad.

Young George got an education in Uniontown. When, in 1954, he rededicated the French and Indian War fort constructed by colonial militia in the mountains six miles east of town, he spoke of his early days. He recalled a family picnic along the banks of a nearby stream and his father's stirring account of the battle of Fort Necessity: an adventurous tale of Red Coats and Indians, of Braddock's ill-fated mission and untimely death, and of a certain brave young commander, George Washington. Young George's imagination was set on fire.

On another occasion he noted "that the countryside where I lived had all the beauty of rich, rolling country and nearby mountains. I was always fond of the open field and spent a great deal of my free time fishing and hunting, and it was here and not in school ... that I first came into contact with the history which later lead me into careful searches after the facts of great events which impinged ... on Pennsylvania and which deeply affected the history of the world."

With his father and friends, Marshall often hunted pheasant and grouse along the worn path of Braddock's Trail. He fished in the small stream that crosses next to the high sheltering boulders from which Washington directed fire on a French contingent led by Ensign Jumonville. He was familiar with the "bald knob" that was Dunbar's camp, where, as Marshall explained, "Colonel Dunbar of Braddock's command ignominiously buried his ammunition and retired to Philadelphia, leaving the western frontier at the mercy of the French and Indians."

The impact of these associations on Marshall is incalculable. He told the Pennsylvania Society that they "stimulated my interest, first, as a boy, in what actually had happened and later, as a man, in just why it happened and what might have been done to change to better advantage the course of human progress in this turbulent world."

In 1957, Marshall recalled to his official biographer: "In this life of Uniontown you might say I saw the end of an era, because it was a very simple life and a very charming life and had a long history behind it. The families went back to the days of George Washington. ... The coal and coke oven my father operated was right across from the Washington farm... And there was this great life of the nation that flowed through the National Pike and stopped overnight at the (White Swan) Inn, just two blocks beyond the house I lived in as a boy."

"I'm always a little surprised," Marshall continued, "when I think of all the various places I showed up at in Uniontown when I was a boy. As far as I could figure out, I seem to have stuck my nose into everything."

He saw the town develop. The streetcar came to town. He was fourteen or so, and said, "I was as fascinated with that as the other boys in town were." He recalled the paving of Main Street and the fact that his father - to his great regret - made him hose down both sides of the street in front of the Marshall home before he left for school in the morning.

He recalled the first long-distance telephones in

town: a bank of some twenty telephones placed on a single board for demonstration purposes. George called Chicago. He recalled the parade of circus trains, and local baseball teams so good they occasionally played traveling professional teams and won. George himself played football and baseball, though he was limited by a weak arm in baseball and a slender build in football.

He remembered rushing from home to the train station early one morning to buy the newspaper for the account of the John L. Sullivan-James Corbett heavyweight championship fight. "Later on," he said, "when the telegraph would give the news of fights, I remember waiting outside the telegraph office where they read the messages aloud to us."

He remembered loafing at the neighborhood blacksmith shop, and bicycling - out to the Thompson farm on Route 21 with its "beautiful barn" (farm house and barn are still there, next to the Springdale Golf Course), and on one occasion to Brownsville. There he and his friends boarded a boat for New Geneva, where Swiss artisans, expert in glass-making, fascinated the red-haired, freckle-faced youngster known as Flicker.

He remembered his friends: his best friend

Andy Thompson, the son of J.V.; Bill Wood, whose father owned a harness shop; Jim Conrad, a chum at school; Herbert Bowman, the future great athlete at Yale, expert alike in baseball and football; Ed Hustead, whose father, Captain Hustead, was a Civil War veteran and commander of cavalry troops at the battle of New Market, Virginia, where the cadets of the Virginia Military Institute had emblazoned their names in glory; Lida Nichols, the future queen of Thorn and Taxis, a European principality; and the Lindsey sisters, Catherine and Nannie. Young George was devoted to Catherine, pretty, scholarly, unapproachable. Trying to impress her, he assiduously studied his spelling words one school session, made his way to the top of the class, only to fail on the last go-around of the spelling bee. Humiliated, he returned to "the bottom," never to attempt again so daunting an undertaking.

There were other friends as well: Haskells and Ewings and Kennedys, Gadds and Meads and Gilmores - all familiar and important names in Fayette County's coal and coke era.

Andy Thompson and George Marshall were "inseparable" as boys. One story concerns their outfitting a raft to transport schoolmates across Coal Lick Run. The boys took their "business" seriously, even devising tickets for the ferry operation. One day a group of girls refused to hand over their tickets. George, with his hat pulled on backward to look like a real ferry pilot, was humiliated. To get even he pulled the cork in the bottom of the flatbed boat. A stream of water shot up, and in seconds the girls were wading ashore, soaked and angry enough to tattle on George and Andy. But George had had his revenge. "I'll never forget that," he said, "because I had to do something - and I had to think quickly - and what I did set me up again as the temporary master of the situation."

George and Andy were mischievous types. They once sold corn-silk cigars and beer out of the Marshall basement until George's father closed the business after sampling the brew and seizing "the whole issue," a development the boys very much regretted. On another occasion, they opened a restaurant. They enjoyed great success until

Andy, the cook, seasoned the sweet potatoes with sand.

They seemed always to have some enterprise going. The boys started a greenhouse on the site of an old family barn that had been torn down. The ground, covered with layers of manure, was perfect for planting, with the result that tomatoes ripened to some unusual sizes. Soon the boys were selling their tomatoes to a local grocer who, in turn, sold to an exclusive clientele. The boys were urged by Mr. Marshall to raise their price. Predictably, the grocer balked and, it is believed, stopped ordering. But George and Andy were beyond caring. They had sent a photograph of their tomatoes next to a silver dollar to the Peter Henderson & Company seed firm and received the reply that the tomatoes were the largest company officials had ever seen.

On another occasion, the boys got into the forget-me-not business, selling wild flowers picked from a nearby field and planted in painted strawberry boxes garlanded with layers of moss. The whole package was sold to the girls at school for an "infinitesimal" sum. Then one day one of their classmates discovered the forget-me-nots could be gotten for free simply by walking a short distance from home. Afterward, George said, "We were boycotted. ... But it taught us a little bit about the middleman in business."

At least once the boys courted trouble with the law. George Gadd, whose blacksmith shop facing "a great cobblestone square" on South Street became the West End boys' clubhouse, interested George and Andy in the "sport" of fighting chickens. Even then, cock fighting posed certain moral and legal problems, though the boys seemed oblivious to any and all difficulties.

Indeed, George and Andy were hell-bent in their new pursuit. They even managed to deceive George's mother, who asked for a demonstration. At first, Mrs. Marshall was "much opposed" to the boys' activity, believing, apparently, all the stories she had heard about the bloody sport. In order to show her it wasn't awful at all, George and Andy staged a "fight" in which two bantams, minus steel spurs, looked "cute and didn't hurt one another." The deception worked like a dream.

From small fighting chickens the boys graduated to larger and more vicious ones. Soon George and Andy were eager to enter their prize fighters in the cock fights conducted in the mountains east of Uniontown. Attended by Pittsburgh swells and sports, these fights occasionally attracted the interest of the law.

Whether George and Andy considered this a real obstacle is unknown. What gave them pause was their age. Two boys so young would not be permitted to enter the cockfighting ring. So they enlisted the older Gadd. With the blacksmith primed and with several "very good chickens" in tow, the boys hitched up a horse to a two-wheeled cart and wound their way up the mountain. In position at the cockfights they mapped out an escape route - just in case.

The mountains were thick with Pittsburgh men, forty or fifty crowded into a tight circle placing bets. Then the improbable happened. Police officers were suddenly everywhere. Terrified, the boys "just squirted out of the forest." Unfortunately, the two confederates went in opposite directions.

George spent the remainder of the day hiding. Finally, with the woods quiet and apparently deserted, he "began in Indian fashion trying ... to get out of there." When he spotted a "shadow," he "scouted" it for more than hour. The "shadow" did the same to George. It was Andy.

Finally rendezvousing, the boys began the long, arduous nighttime journey down the mountainside. At one in the morning they reached home. George, fearful that a false step would wake his father, tiptoed into his room. His mother appeared almost immediately. George told his story. So outlandish and even ridiculous were parts of it that Laura Marshall laughed till she cried.

And afterward there were no reprimands or punishment. In a 1952 letter, Marshall remembered his mother as "both gentle and firm, very understanding, and had a keen but quiet sense of humor, which made her my confidant in practically all my boyish escapades and difficulties."

Besides, he said, "if I told her I realized I was wrong ... there was no use her telling me it was wrong."

1896: The July 4th Parade at 5-Corners

George needed all the help he could get from his mother. She seems to have provided it unstintingly. Once, George and Andy got into a bit of a jam when a "holdup" they staged went awry.

Imitating a local mountain gang they had read about, the boys high tailed it out of town one day, hid themselves in the bushes along the side of a road, and when a carriage or farmer's buggy passed, would jump out behind the vehicle and shoot BBs in its direction. It was great fun until they fired at a buggy that was minus the small glass window that should have shielded the driver's head and neck. George and Andy let go with a perfect bull's-eye volley, hit the farmer in the neck, and then ran as fast as they could, with the injured party in hot pursuit. Coming to a fence too high to climb they rolled underneath, while the farmer, a good deal older than the boys, could only manage to watch and stare.

Frightened, George and Andy lingered awhile, and then figured out a "disguise." They simply turned their coats inside out and placed their hats on backward. Surely, now, they were inconspicuous. They made their way home.

Mrs. Marshall was the first to spot the two fugitives. She thought the boys' camouflaged appearance simply hilarious; the "tragic" circumstances surrounding the boys' dilemma failed to impress her. She decided, though, not to tell a soul what had happened, and even extended a sort of benevolent protection to George and Andy, shielding them for the next two or three days from whatever "embarrassing" questions might arise.

As George later recalled: "Sometimes (Mother) may have been worried; sometimes she may even have been ashamed; sometimes she may have been shocked; but she heard what the matter was ... and whenever there was any humor in it, it amused her very much."

Young George had little difficulty finding mischief - with or without Andy's help. Not even church attendance could shelter him. Indeed, on at least one occasion it proved his downfall. Sunday mornings the Marshalls attended St. Peter's Episcopal Church on Morgantown Street. Here, George's job was to "pump" the organ for the organist, Miss Fannie Howe, a prim and proper matron whose sense of duty was acute.

"The pumping was not difficult except you have to be there," Marshall later said. "But there were long periods of waiting during the sermon. On one of these mornings I was occupying this period by reading a five-cent novel of that day by Nick Carter.

"Just in the most exciting portion ... my attention was called to the organ by the thump, thump ... Miss Howe would make from the keyboard. I realized that she had started to play at the end of the sermon and no music was coming out. So I pumped the organ very hurriedly."

Naturally, Miss Howe was outraged, and following the service fired George. Though the experience was painful for the young man, it was not as painful as what awaited him at home. And it didn't help matters that the Nick Carter books were forbidden to George. Normally, they were read, alone, in the springhouse in the backyard, never in the house and never, never in church.

Sometimes trouble just seemed to follow

George around. This was the case one summer afternoon when sister Marie played host to some girls from the private school she attended. Marie and the young ladies were enjoying themselves on the Marshall's back porch. George, banished from the house, was across the street in Andy's backyard. George, Andy, and Herb Bowman were there engaged in the celebrated art of swatting bees with a paddle. One pesky critter got George to hop around, stinging him at "the hairline" until the youngster could no longer stand it and bolted away. In a flash, he swept past Andy's house and crossed Main Street at a gallop. He was headed straight to the Marshall front door, with the bee in pursuit. Inside the house George made a sharp right turn. The bee, however, continued a straight flight in the direction of the girls. Marie was furious.

George's "last licking" involved his sister and a case of mistaken identity. Marie, it seems, was at an upstairs window "jeering" as George hosed down Main Street in front of the house. It was a job George detested, and to have his sister taunt him doubled the embarrassment. With his back turned, he heard the front door open. George whirled and sent a blast of water in that direction. There was a scream. George, startled, saw that it was his mother. Too late. She was already soaked. "She was shocked but very much amused," George reported years later, for she "knew the terrible plight I was in, which arrived shortly with my father."

It was a difficult time for the whole family. The national economic depression of 1893 wiped out Mr. Marshall's savings as well as a promising real estate deal. Having invested heavily in a Virginia land deal, he was forced to sell at a substantial loss. Afterward, the family took desperate measures. George's transfer out of private school was part of this. So was "the very painful and humiliating" experience of carrying home table scraps for Towser and the other family dogs from the kitchen of a hotel close to home. "I didn't enjoy it at all," George said, "It was always sort of a black mark on my boyhood."

The family recovered, slowly. Mr. Marshall either managed to retain control of his Dunbar holdings or to buy them back, and George returned to private school. The family was never free of worry, however. George's allowance as a VMI cadet was $5 a month. Following his sophomore year, his mother informed him that he might not be able to return to school, as the family was, once again, practically broke. The threatened insolvency never occurred, thanks to Mrs. Marshall, who managed to sell off some parcels of real estate she owned in Pittsburgh.

Weathering these lean years, Mrs. Marshall emerged as the family caretaker. "She was in poor health," George would recall, "yet she did all the work of our home and made it a cheerful place."

George loved his mother (as well as his sister). He loved his father, too, but as his official biographer put it, he was "also a little afraid of him."

His attitude toward his brother was more complex. Older than George by a half dozen years, Stuart Marshall had been a brilliant student at VMI. Trained as a chemist, he pursued a scientific career of more than modest success. Even as adults, however, the Marshall brothers did not get along.

Early on there were the normal tag-along episodes brothers engage in. Once, after a National Guard encampment close to home, Stuart and his friends, imbued with the military spirit, decided to set up their own camp on the opposite side of the creek, close to a steep bank. Stuart very much wanted to bivouac alone with his chums, but his mother had a different idea. George would go, too.

Later that night, while George dozed inside a tent, the rest of the garrison fled in a headlong rush, falling into the creek to save themselves. The attacker, George revealed many years later, was a cow that had evidently overrun the boys' skirmish line. Back in the house, safe and secure, Stuart had to admit to his parents that George was among the missing. Mr. Marshall was perfectly furious, for a change, at Stuart. He ordered the boy back across the creek with him. There they found George snoozing, oblivious to danger.

It is possible that a succession of such incidents might have soured the boys' relationship. Then, too, there was the gap in their ages. Six years is a big spread between siblings. Otherwise, it's difficult to see why either boy had cause for complaint. As a child, George got most everything he wanted, and at Christmas received the lion's share of gifts. As for Stuart, he was the adored "star" of the family, the most brilliant and gifted of the Marshall children.

Whatever the cause of the brothers' falling out, it is clear the crisis between them worked to George's advantage, although that seemed improbable at the time. If only Stuart had better appreciated his brother; he completely underestimated George and failed to recognize his brother's innate abilities, his drive, and determination.

An episode occurred just as George was applying to enter VMI, at the age of sixteen, in 1897. Stuart left no doubt where he stood on the matter. Speaking with his mother in private, Stuart begged his parents not to send George, arguing that his brother could not possibly make the grade and would, in time, blacken the family name and diminish his own considerable reputation for scholastic excellence.

George overheard. He recalled, "I decided right then and there I was going to 'wipe my brother's eye.'" What his parents and teachers could not accomplish, Stuart had. "I became the senior cadet officer. I was Captain of the Corps, so I finally got ahead of what my brother had done. The urgency came from hearing that conversation my brother had with my mother. It had quite a psychological effect on my career."

In just about every other way, George Marshall's boyhood was perfect. The Marshall backyard was made for a rough and ready youngster. There was the stream, Coal Lick Run, the barn and later the greenhouse, what the family called the "orchard," a carriage house, four large apple trees, the brick springhouse, "a very crude shack" where George's rabbits stayed, and right outside his bedroom window, off the porch on the second floor, a grape vine that wrapped around a gigantic maple tree. This arrangement allowed George, on pleasant summer mornings, to "step out of bed and walk in my bare feet on the porch and pull down bunches of delicious Concord grapes."

George Marshall Sr., despite being somewhat

The Marshall Home On West Main

severe at home (it was an unusual Victorian-era father who wasn't), was gregarious and really quite engaging. A Democrat and a Mason, and popular about town, it is clear from the record that Mr. Marshall would have done anything for his children, including George. Fishing once in the nearby mountains, Mr. Marshall "delayed" catching any fish at all in order to help George reel in catch after catch, "thirty bass in all." It was a day George would never forget.

One winter the Marshalls bought their youngest son his very own Flexible Flyer sled. Thereafter, George and his father rode together, Mr. Marshall's wide girth adding to the sled's weight and velocity. "I sat in the front with a skate on my foot (to guide the sled) and my father would sit behind and was supposed to swing the sled," George recalled. On snowy evenings, with all the boys and fathers from the West End shouting with delight, the Marshalls would barrel down the icy roadway, desperate to hang on as the sled took "jumpers," bumps in the street at sidewalk intersections.

George liked people. He made friends at the only black-owned barber shop in town. He became acquainted with visiting circus "barkers." He loafed at Kramer's store, purchasing penny candies and swapping tales with friends. At the Thompson farm, west of Uniontown, George did chores alongside the regular farmhands, a hardy group of men who reminded the youngster of the cowboys he read about in his favorite dime-store novels. "They were always tearing down a fellow and making little of him to the immense amusement of all the others," he reported. George helped in the barn, hauling hay and distributing manure.

Shortly after becoming Chief of Staff in 1939, General Marshall appeared before a congressional panel considering Army appropriations. The congressmen were naturally curious about this new top man, especially his past ties to Capitol Hill. The General smiled and told them how, as a boy, his local congressman had mailed him a packet of seeds. George promptly planted the seeds, but after a long wait nothing happened. All in all, the seeds would have done better several hundred miles south of Uniontown. Western Pennsylvania, he told the lawmakers, was not exactly "cotton" country. The committee members, he recalled, were "much amused," especially by his facetious declaration that the cotton seed incident had "been enough for me" and, as a result, he hadn't bothered with Congress since.

George's youthful political experiences were limited, but by no means negligible. In this, as in other matters, Marshall Sr. was a major influence. Like Mr. Marshall, George was a Democrat. At least he marched in Democratic torch light parades. George's fondest political memory was a nighttime march on behalf of the Democratic candidate for president in 1896, William Jennings Bryan: he carried a Democratic cane and a Bryan hat - a gray fedora. George's first political lesson occurred in a gubernatorial election. That year's torch light parade was a tumultuous affair, a "tremendous to-do," George said. Later, when the results came in, the candidate whose election appeared to be a sure thing came up the loser, falling victim to "the political organization of the city of Philadelphia" and that city's "controlled vote."

As he grew older, George's interest in public affairs became more evident. Between his sophomore and juniors years at VMI, the young cadet secured a job with the National Geological Survey mapping the area around Uniontown. The summer of 1899 was significant because the United States was engaged in a bitter struggle in the Philippines. Having defeated the Spanish, U.S. soldiers were locked in fierce combat against the "insurrectos," Filipinos anxious to secure their island's complete independence.

All of Uniontown followed with intense interest the news from far-off Manila. The 10th Pennsylvania Regiment included Company C, composed of men from Uniontown, the surrounding countryside, and nearby villages. Though few residents of the city had known the location of the Philippine Islands before the unit's departure in April 1898, the battles the men were soon waging galvanized every citizen. News cables and letters reaching Uniontown telling of casualties and individual acts of courage by the hometown boys heightened matters to a fever pitch.

The town's preparation for Company C's return in August 1899 was dazzling. Uniontown, the newspaper said, was "to be smothered by the stars and stripes." Main Street was painted red, white, and blue. Four thousand yards of bunting and over a thousand flags were displayed. Six tall arches were erected at key street locations. One arch was made of coal, another was bedecked with one hundred electric lights. Ornamental swords were ordered for the officers, medals for the enlisted men. The celebration was to be capped by a gigantic parade, a sumptuous fete, and all-day free activities at the Uniontown fairgrounds. Every citizen was expected to attend. The whole town would turn out.

President McKinley, welcoming the soldiers to Pittsburgh days earlier, gave voice to the feelings of local citizens almost perfectly when he declared of the 10th Regiment's Philippine service: "No finer instance of heroic and self-sacrificing patriotism has been known in the history of our country."

On the day of the parade, August 29, 1899, George Marshall secured a place for himself along the parade route. The ninety eight men and three officers of Company C arrived at 1:08 p.m. at the railroad station on Gallatin Avenue. They stepped off into a cauldron of noise and excitement. Preceded by marching Civil War veterans, the company made a circular route through town. The men marched up Main Street, turned left at Morgantown Street, pivoted left again onto Fayette Street, caught Wilson Avenue, made a right turn at Jefferson, moved along Shady Lane back to Main, halting finally on Pittsburgh Street.

"With patriotic shot and booming cannon, San Francisco welcomed the boys to their country; Pittsburgh will welcome them to their state; and it remains for us to welcome them to their home," declared retired Captain John H. Campbell days before.

This they did. And although the country was divided over the war and its imperial role in the Philippines, the town itself was united in its tribute to the men of Company C - as Marshall observed half a century later - on their "return with the honors of war." "No man could make a purchase," Marshall recalled. "The town was his."

The parade of Company C was Marshall's "first great emotional reaction." Not even the victory parades in Paris and London in 1919, in which he participated as an aide to General John J. Pershing, surpassed the "individual excitement" of the Uniontown homecoming. Later, he recognized the celebration as "a grand American small-town demonstration of pride in its young men and of wholesome enthusiasms over their achievements."

It pointed, he said, toward the role the United States would play in the 20th century. For nineteen-year-old George Marshall the return of Company C was confirmation, as well as acclamation. He would have an Army career. In retirement, he said: "I've sometimes thought that the impressions of that period, and particularly of that parade, had a determining effect on my choice of a profession." Marshall grew to manhood at a time when America was assuming new responsibilities. In August 1899, George witnessed the majesty of arms. In Uniontown, he saw heroism wedded to purpose, and joy in the faces of the people.

What sort of young man left Uniontown to return

as General, as Secretary of State, as Nobel Peace laureate? Historian Forrest Pogue noted, "It is clear he got from (his hometown) a thorough grounding in the American tradition." Indeed, George Marshall emerged from youth strong and resolute in character, interested in the world, inquisitive, and ready to succeed.

He had backbone. This was evident early. Before joining the Army, he traveled to Washington to get the political backing that was needed in those days to take the examination required of would-be first lieutenants. He took with him his father's calling card, with which he met Secretary of State Philander Knox. Knox, of Brownsville, ostensibly a friend of George's father, was unable or unwilling to help the young man. George then made a bold decision: he would go to the White House, unannounced, and petition President McKinley directly.

At the mansion, the second-floor butler inquired whether he had an appointment. Marshall said he didn't. Well, the butler answered, you won't get in.

But George saw the President. After waiting hours, he "attached" himself to a party of three - a father, mother and daughter - who were there to shake hands with the chief executive. After they bowed out, George remained.

President McKinley politely asked what the young man wanted. George, all of twenty-one, told him.

Audacious? Of course. But that was Marshall's nature. It wasn't any more daring than Colonel Marshall, many years later, defending the performance of tired American troops to an astonished General Pershing early in World War I. Or telling Franklin Roosevelt, at one of their first meetings, that the President was dead wrong to believe that airpower alone could carry the day against the Germans and the Japanese. On both occasions, fellow-officers bade Marshall farewell, certain that he had angered and most probably alienated the man in charge. On both occasions, Marshall not only stayed but was entrusted with greater responsibility.

Sometimes, it is possible to hear distinct echoes of the Uniontown years in Marshall's career. There was one such incident in the

Philippines during his first overseas assignment. Lieutenant George Marshall was leading his men across a swampy stream when one of the soldiers yelled, "Crocodile." This panicked the rest of the troops, and in the process of going slightly berserk, the lot of them nearly drowned Marshall. To get to the opposite bank as quickly as possible, they stomped on their lieutenant's back, sending him to the bottom.

Marshall faced roughly the same challenge he had confronted as ferry boat conductor years earlier, when the girls of Uniontown had refused to hand over their tickets to him. Then he had pulled the plug in the bottom of the boat and sent the girls splashing to shore. Determined, instinctive action was again the order of the day, and Marshall took it, knowing it "wasn't the time for cussing around."

"I got up to the top, I took my position in front of them," he later reported, "wet and covered with mud, and fell them in very formally. I then gave them 'right shoulder arms,' facing them down into the stream and clear to the other side. As they reached the other bank, I gave them 'to the rear, march.' They came back up out of the crocodile stream. ... Then we started on our excursion up into the mountains there, trying to find the insurrecto holdout."

Marshall, as he himself put it, was once again "master of the situation."

The General and J. Buell Snyder at Connellsville Airport

The Hero Returns

Two silvery aircraft descended from the sky in the blazing heat of Saturday, September 10, 1939. At 2 o'clock in the afternoon a seventeen gun salute reverberated across the concrete runway of the new Connellsville Airport. Emerging from one of the planes (both planes were two engine military aircraft, but the first on the ground carried a civilian Congressman Buell Snyder) was a ruddy-faced, fifty-nine-year-old U.S. Army general resplendent in an all-white, summer-dress uniform. A small cluster of ribbons rode above his left breast pocket. He carried himself with unusual reserve. But he was smiling. He could hardly help himself. There were ten thousand people on hand to give him a rousing welcome. This was his day; officially, "George Marshall Day" in Fayette County.

He had been back before, of course. How many times is hard to say. It is evident, from photographs, that George attended at least one family outing between his departure for the

Philippines in 1902 and his father's death in 1909. It is probable that he showed the town off to his wife, Lilly. Following Lilly's early death due to heart failure and his remarriage, George stopped briefly in the company of his second wife, Katherine, in the late summer or early fall of 1938. In the family Pontiac, George and Katherine motored from Fire Island, New York, to Washington, D.C., and then over the mountains to Uniontown. Their ultimate destination was Chicago, where George's duties included command of Civilian Conservation Corps camps. Marshall was now a brigadier general; his name would soon come up for consideration as deputy chief of staff, one step from the top rung.

This 1938 visit was fateful. It was the last meeting between George and his closest friend from childhood, Andy Thompson. They were virtual strangers now. There had been a reunion, years before, at which Andy had acted rather imperious toward George. Despite his father's financial setbacks, Andy Thompson had restored part of the family's fortune, though by no means on the scale of J.V.'s early successes.

George, meanwhile, appeared stuck in an army career of no great note, despite his outstanding service with General John J. Pershing during and after World War I, headlines praising his military acumen at the Meuse-Argonne (where he had deftly supervised the movement of six hundred thousand troops to the front lines), and his later service at Ft. Benning, where he practically rewrote the Army textbook on infantry warfare, stressing movement and quick calculation of an enemy's weak spots rather than the static defenses of old. But these were achievements not especially noteworthy in the 1920s and 1930s. America got fed up pretty quickly following the Armistice with the whole idea of the World War and international responsibility. If Andy was like most Americans, he hardly gave the military passing notice; he may have thought that life, meaning civilian life, had passed George by. Poor George. He had wasted himself.

But it was Andy who should have been pitied. On October 18, 1938, three days after Marshall's appointment as deputy chief of staff, Andy was dead, along with his brother, John, under circumstances never adequately explained. George didn't attend Andy's funeral service in Franklin, Pennsylvania, hundreds of miles north of his youthful haunts and business successes. There, in his wife's hometown, Andy Thompson was laid to rest.

In a way, George might very well have agreed with a negative assessment of his career. Long years of outstanding service but without any clear route to advancement frustrated and even angered him. In those days, the Army was a hidebound organization and slow to reward talent. Everything was "by the book," meaning an officer waited his turn in the molasses of seniority. Marshall once ruefully joked that "colonels of the infantry of the Regular Army" are of course "high-minded and seriously employed." He was then senior instructor attached to the Illinois National Guard. It was the depth of the Depression, 1933, and the chief reason he was in Chicago, with its army of unemployed and hungry men, was to prepare the Guard for possible "internal" difficulties, labor unrest and the like.

Marshall was deeply troubled by the country's

plight during the years of the Great Depression. He lamented the waste of good men, and his own relative impotence. He wrote a friend, "Whenever I am conniving to get these young (officers) with genuine ability put into a suitable setting, I deplore the fact that I have not gained a position of sufficient power to do what I think should be done. I am awfully tired of seeing mediocrity placed in high positions, with brilliance and talent damned by rank to obscurity. There are so many junior officers of tremendous ability whose qualities the service is losing all advantage of that it is really tragic."

Tragic was a word that could have been applied to his own career. Brilliant in many respects, his admirers feared he would be forever condemned to the endless treadmill of Army life. The glittering prize of Army chief of staff, and with it the capacity to influence events, still seemed far off in the early 1930s.

In fact, Marshall waited thirty five years to achieve his first general's star. When his time finally came, in the late summer of 1939, his old mentor and boss, General Pershing, was able to write Mrs. Marshall: "George's appointment has met with universal approval. ... He is in a position where he will make a great name for himself and prove a great credit to the American Army and the American people."

Pershing, the great hero of the World War, had been one of his chief backers; so too had been Harry Hopkins, a close aide and friend to the President. Unexpected help came from Senator Joseph Guffey of Pennsylvania, his sister Marie's friend from Greensburg. Marshall had called on the senator in his Capitol Hill office and later reported Guffey was "all excited. I had the damnedest time to keep him from seeing the President. I said you will destroy me. Let things take their course and maybe I will get it."

A combination of factors propelled Marshall to the top: Luck, persistence, some artful politicking, and the unsuitability of other contenders. To no small degree Marshall became chief of staff because of the record he had built over the years and because of a stellar reputation. He was acquainted with a great many people and a great many situations. As he himself noted in a letter to one of his boosters, "The National Guard knows me. The Reserve Corps knows me well. The ROTC people, including many college presidents, know me. And the regular Army knows me."

Only the American public seemed unaware of him.

In the crisis atmosphere of the late 1930s that wouldn't take long to remedy. The Munich episode in the fall of 1938, in which Great Britain had bargained away Czechoslovakia at a peace conference with the German Fuhrer Adolf Hitler, started the country down the path to war.

Unlike the Munich crisis, which caught official Washington off guard, the actual start of hostilities in September 1939 was greeted with a certain forbearance and grim determination. At the White House, President Roosevelt directed that a map of the battlefront be placed over the mantel in the Oval Office. Beginning Saturday, September 3, officials, including the new Army chief of staff George Marshall, had been at their battle stations, or at the White House for conferences with the commander-in-chief.

Five days after the outbreak of hostilities, prompted by the German invasion of Poland, the President signed an executive order increasing Army and Navy strength. Secretary of War Harry Woodring announced the Army would boost enlistments by seventeen thousand men, raising total strength to two hundred and twenty-seven thousand men, the figure which, under law, the Army would have attained by July 1940. Still, the Army was woefully undermanned and outgunned by the European armies now taking the field. The United States boasted the nineteenth largest army in the world, between Portugal and Bulgaria. Germany had more than six million men trained and ready for war. The Nazi regime was on its way to fielding 136 divisions by May 1940; the United States would be able to count on only five divisions.

From the very first, Marshall established himself as the primary advocate of Army expansion. In November 1938, Roosevelt had summoned Marshall to the White House along with some other top advisors: Henry Morgenthau, Harry Hopkins, Louis Johnson and Generals Malin Craig and Henry "Hap" Arnold. The President did most of the talking, and all of it was about how he wanted to increase the size of the Army Air Corps by ten- or twenty-thousand new planes. The gist of FDR's remarks was that this new firepower would demonstrate U.S. resolve and perhaps frighten Hitler. Forget about ground forces and new rifles or even barracks for that matter, the President said. The airplane is the thing.

After speaking, Roosevelt went around the room for reaction to his plan. He turned to Marshall with a jaunty, "Don't you think so, George?" Unaccustomed to being addressed so casually by someone he barely knew, the deputy chief of staff shot the President a frosty stare, and replied, "I am sorry, Mr. President, but I don't agree with that at all."

Now, in September 1939, Marshall was summoned again. The President and the General were growing accustomed to one another. Roosevelt knew that Marshall would speak his mind. The truth might be painful at times. "Is that all right?" Marshall had asked on one occasion. The

President, whose habit was to agree with everyone and to smile frequently, nodded. "You said yes pleasantly, but it may be unpleasant," Marshall warned.

In fact, what Marshall had in mind all along was an Army strengthened in all its parts; ground, air, artillery, tank units. Marshall didn't know exactly the face of modern warfare, but he knew enough to realize that tanks and trucks were revolutionizing the art of war-making. He realized as well that the Army was starting far back. During one of his many trips to Capitol Hill, the General noted that whereas a battalion in any other man's army was made up of eight hundred to a thousand men, the average U.S. Army battalion was composed of two hundred men, "including cooks, clerks, and kitchen police."

Marshall would not get all that he wanted - not at first anyway. The seventeen-thousand-man increase in Army strength was accompanied, on September 8, by a presidential proclamation of limited emergency. The President declared that "there is no thought in any shape, manner, or form of putting the nation, either in its defenses or in its internal economy, on a war basis. That is the one thing we are going to avoid. We are going to keep the nation on a peace basis, in accordance with peacetime authorization."

In private, the President counseled the Army chief of staff that the small military expansion he had called for "was all the public would be ready to accept without undue excitement."

Not since the fevered meetings of April 1917 had Washington seen anything like this. Even before the first crash of German guns, Undersecretary of State Sumner Welles and his counterpart at the Treasury, John Wesley Hanes, convened a meeting of what *Time* magazine subsequently dubbed the "council of preparedness." The conferees included Marshall, Assistant Secretary of War Louis Johnson, Assistant Attorney General Thurman Arnold, Navy Secretary Thomas Edison, and the Chief of Naval Operations Harold Stark. On the 2nd of September, the President called a meeting at the White House. Afterward, a *New York Times* photographer framed the participants in his lens. War Secretary Stimson anchored the left side of the picture; at the right hand side stood General Marshall, dressed in a civilian suit, his obligatory form of attire owing to public and Congressional suspicion of soldiers, especially generals, in uniform.

More meetings followed, and on Thursday, the 8th, the *Army and Navy Journal* reported that President Roosevelt was forming a "high command" composed of himself, Secretary of State Cordell Hull, Secretary of War Woodring, Admiral Stark, and General Marshall.

It was stated that "to that (high command) authority will go all matters relating to national defense, and without interfering with the Cabinet, it will develop those means and determine those measures which are essential to promote and protect our vital interests."

Adding credence to the report, the *Journal* stated, and the *New York Times* repeated on September 9, that General Marshall, in order to meet in Washington over the weekend, had canceled a "speaking engagement scheduled for tomorrow in Uniontown, Pa."

Perhaps the *Army and Navy Journal* was flat wrong about the Uniontown trip; perhaps the President thought it was best that his top advisors go about their business with no cancellations of long-standing commitments, the better not to alarm the nation; or perhaps Marshall himself made the decision to fly from steamy Washington to the blistering tarmac at the Connellsville airport, there to be greeted by a crowd of ten thousand

It was an occasion both solemn and joyful. There was a receiving line, and the Connellsville High School band, and the introduction of Miss Kay Wilson of Alabama, airplane hostess and the officially designated Miss America of the Airways. Mrs. Marshall and Marshall's stepdaughter, Molly Brown, were also on hand along with Marie, in from Greensburg, with her doctor husband, John Singer.

The formal receiving line was largely composed of old friends like tall, dapper O'Neil Kennedy, editor of the Democratic-leaning *Morning Herald*. Before the ceremonies and the motorcade got under way, however, the General was awash in a sea of informality. Famed local baseball pitcher Harry Wilhelm shook Marshall's hand, and the chief of staff later remarked that Wilhelm "could zip 'em over the plate." Isaac Silverman, an old chum, took the General's hand, pumped it, and while speaking, fixed Marshall with a most sincere gaze.

Politics was not to be avoided, and the exercise at the airport had something of the air of a tribute to Congressmen Snyder, whose importance to Marshall, incidentally, was clear: Snyder chaired the House committee that controlled military appropriations. Colonel Edgar S. Gorrell, president of the Air Transport Association of America, was on hand to praise the congressman for his efforts on behalf of the airport, indicating the county as a result had unlimited possibilities, "vertically speaking." Colonel William E.R. Covell of the Army Corps of Engineers lauded Snyder for his attempts to secure a $10 million appropriation to control flooding on the Youghiogheny River, one part of which would be the construction of a dam.

It took Congressman Snyder to get back to the point of the ceremony, declaring, "the United States is indeed fortunate in having the type of man as George Marshall as the head of the U.S. Armies." Judge E.H. Reppert, of the welcoming committee, stated that "in this hour of menace, it adds to our sense of security to know that George

Marshall is in a position to preserve the safety of America and its institutions." Like the congressman, Judge Reppert was hazarding a guess.

These ceremonies marked the conclusion of a harrowing nine day period for Marshall. He had taken the oath as chief of staff and witnessed the start of a war whose shape and form, and possible meaning for the United States, were by no means certain. But as he stepped to the platform he wanted the people - *his* hometown people - to know that "if war comes, the United States is ready."

The course of events would, he continued, be decided by statesmen and politicians. For a reading of the future it would be best if declarations came from them, and not from a soldier like himself. Nevertheless, speaking for the Army, Marshall noted "we are moving along ... taking steps which seem advisable in view of the troubled situation abroad." In any case, he added, "we are in a more fortunate position than we were in 1917, and it gives me great confidence."

Looking out across the throng, perhaps the largest ever assembled in the county to greet one individual, General Marshall declared, "We are a fortunate people in the United States. We are blessed with freedom and happiness ... fortunate beyond the fondest hopes and dreams of any people in any country in Europe, and we must be careful in the preservation of our good fortune."

The motorcade was ready to roll. First up was Connellsville. From there, Marshall and his party drove to the mountains, probably through Dunbar, where his father's first business had been located. Then it was on to Uniontown, where a reception was held starting at 5 p.m. at the home of Dr. and Mrs. Charles Smith of 93 Morgantown Street.

At some point the General managed a visit to his old Uniontown neighborhood. Remarking on the occasion nearly two decades later, the General complained that "I couldn't remember anything. They had buried my youthful associations under a twenty-foot landfill." It was true. The Marshall home had long ago given way to the West End Theater and to the high embankment of Coal Lick Run. The chief of staff had a better experience across the street at the old Thompson homestead. Here, in his youth, was located a springhouse and twenty paces away a honey locust tree. Between the two "ran a deep trail," he recalled, "and a continuous procession of ants going or coming to the wash house."

Entering the yard, he found much of the landscape changed. Though the honey locust tree remained, the springhouse had been demolished. As for the trail of ants, it was nowhere to be found. An old man sitting on the back porch of an adjacent house observed the General. Finally, the chief of staff asked the old man for an explanation. He was told he was "turned around" about the location of the springhouse. Incredibly, Marshall then discovered the trail of ants "running exactly as it had in my youth so many, many years before."

The uncovering of the ants delighted the General, and he may have then reflected on the fact that if either his parents or Andy's parents had provided the boys with a magnifying glass, their lives might have turned out far differently, for as boys they had been keenly interested in that never-ending procession.

The town knew of the great responsibilities Marshall carried. The hope was expressed that he would "measure up," as *Morning Herald* reporter Mary Kate O'Bryon stated in a quarter-page "Welcome Home" advertisement paid for by Wright-Metzler's department store. But this Uniontown trip was designed as a respite from weighty and substantial matters.

O'Bryon wrote: "Our special welcome is for `Flicker,' the snub-nosed, freckle-faced, red-head who was the natural-born leader of boydom in the West End in the `90s, who coasted on Gilmore's hill, staged shows in Thompson's stable, and kept things generally a-stir. Today, we hope you can lay aside your honors and your burdens and make friends with your youth. 'Flicker' Marshall has been gone for such a long, long time."

Still, there was something infinitely serious about it all, for Marshall himself was treating the occasion as an "almost ceremonial return to the wellsprings of his youth," as Forrest Pogue stated, "as if renewing his strength in preparation for the future."

At the evening banquet, Congressman Snyder reminded the guests of his own support for the lifting of the arms embargo in the Neutrality Act. Wooda Carr, the U.S. postmaster in Uniontown, and the evening's toastmaster, then introduced the guest of honor.

Unbeknownst to Marshall, the ceremony was being broadcast (no doubt thanks to Congressman Snyder, one of the owners of the station) live on WMBS radio, so that his voice reached beyond the four hundred guests at the White Swan Hotel to the whole town and most of the county.

He began by remarking on "old boyhood chums" Andy Thompson, Bill Woods, George Gadd, Frank Lewellyn, and others. He recounted playing "hooky" from school and being found out by his sister. "Dammit all, she's a beloved sister, but I got heck just the same," he said to laughter. He recalled the illegal "game roosters" he and Andy kept and of keeping out of sight of Judge Umbel for this reason, and how the Pittsburgh sports "used to come to town" and how they and some of the townsfolk retreated to the mountains for the fighting "contests."

He pointed out the presence at the banquet of his former teacher, Lee Smith. "He once told me I deserved a licking, and I agreed with him and do so today. I was not a very good student," Marshall said, "but he was kind and considerate and gave me some advice I should have followed. I shall never forget those school days in Uniontown."

The General spoke of his father and of the family picnics beside the little stream in the "great meadow" of Fort Necessity, and of the fact that "right here we had events of world-wide importance. ... What a remarkable thing the events that have occurred in our vicinity - the very spearhead of our American independence."

He spoke of the long-ago parade of Company C of the 10th Pennsylvania Regiment, the Fayette unit that had fought in the Philippines at the turn of the century and had returned to a town bursting with patriotism and pride. "I think it was then that I decided to follow the military part," the General explained, and then, to take the edge off a little: "As I was not a very good student, as my friend Lee Smith can tell you, perhaps it was a good thing I went in for military service."

This was remembrance of a high order, framed, as he said, by "momentous" events, perhaps by the start of a war that might prove more terrible than the Great War. It was "tragic" the events that were unfolding, "very disturbing," and time was not necessarily on the side of the United States. The country had a lot of catching up to do.

But General Marshall was upbeat, confident. He declared that no matter how real the obstacles, the nation would overcome them. "I repeat to you tonight that we have plans, and trained soldiers, and are organized. We have actual leadership of troops. ... There is no confusion, no hurly-burly excitement or hysteria. Everyone knows how to move for whatever defense we find necessary."

This democracy - with its "possibilities (for) peace and happiness ... not enjoyed by other peoples" - will find a way to defend itself in the current world situation. Above all, "We ... must not be misled" or succumb to "emotionalism."

The head of the Army then paused, looked over the audience of old friends and neighbors, and closed by saying:

"I tell you all, I am overjoyed. I am mighty glad to be back home."

Subordinates later spoke of Marshall's icy stare, his reserve and business-like manner. Marshall himself explained he didn't have time to waste. Yet, that's what he appeared to be doing when, as Secretary of State, he invited to his office a delegation of Boy Scouts to learn of their plans to raise money for the starving children of Europe.

The reporters covering the State Department were fit-to-be-tied. There were many pressing matters in 1948 for the Secretary of State to attend to. This was not one of them.

But Marshall was pleased to have the boys there (with reporters present), and while they detailed their plans, he began to mirror his own childhood in the dreams and worldwide ambitions of the scouts. The boys may have been puzzled - Uniontown, Pennsylvania, was surely not on their minds at the start of their day. But Marshall was having the time of his life. Arguably the second most powerful man in the world had discovered a thread binding together the generations.

He said: "I got to thinking at that moment -

just at that moment - of what a contrast that was to my youth. My radius of activity at nine years old didn't go as far as ... Brownsville, which was twelve miles away on the Monongahela. It went up to the mountains because we summered there. But it didn't go over five miles from home.

"I had only heard of Salt Lake as a tale of history. ... I had heard of San Francisco - the Golden Gate -- but that very briefly. I had never heard of Manila - I am quite certain I never had. Pittsburgh was the furthest point, and that was because I was taken there with my mother shopping when she went to 'the city', as they expressed it. ... I described this all to these boys. ... I was rather moved with the whole contrast."

A postscript to General Marshall's visit: in the struggle to rearm, Congressman J. Buell Snyder proved to be a worthwhile partner to the General and the Roosevelt administration. The former public school teacher, a resident of Perryopolis, was an advocate of military expansion months before the bombs fell on Pearl Harbor and the United States was dragged, at long last, into war. As chairman of the committee responsible for voting the money for nearly all of the military's purchases, Snyder traveled widely, boasting once, "I ... visited practically every military post in the continental United States, in the Panama Canal Zone and in our island possessions." In addition, Snyder had "flown in every type of airplane used by our Army Air Corps (and) watched the fabrication of our guns and projectiles at our great manufacturing arsenals."

He professed to see much progress in the years since he and the President had arrived in Washington in 1933, though his words spoken in January 1940, five months after Marshall's return home, were also full of caution and warning. "Our defense program is still in a state of incompletion," he solemnly declared. Believing that Puerto Rico was the lynchpin of our defense of the

Caribbean and the Panama Canal, especially "in these days of aerial and submarine warfare," he called for a buildup of military forces in Puerto Rico as well as in Alaska and along the coastal mainland. The administration's national defense budget represented a "minimum" of what was required, Snyder said. While the President was asking for a 227,000-man peacetime Army, the congressman thought the authorized strength of 280,000 preferable. As for the future, "an addition ... of a full division a year should be made." Though our planes may be the best in the world already, the Congressman favored more and better planes. "In my judgment we should increase our quota of fast pursuit planes and of the improved and powerful long-range bombers of the Flying Fortress type." He wanted improved anti-aircraft protection, and thought "we are still lacking adequate" protection in the skies over the Canal Zone,

Puerto Rico, Hawaii, and "our metropolitan cities."

Congressman Snyder had watched from afar, in September 1939, the destruction of Poland by the German military, but he had formed very definite ideas about U.S. defense as a result. To protect a city like Pittsburgh, he said, it would help to beef up the Air Corps from a projected authorized strength of 6,000 planes to a total of 8,000. He advocated placing "a rim of airports and landing fields" within a 50 to 75 mile radius of major U.S. cities for these planes, and installing "hundreds" of anti-aircraft guns in the vicinity of these airports to protect against sudden attack.

He reasoned, "As perhaps you know, the Poles were wiped out, comparatively speaking, in three days, and one of the chief reasons why the Germans were so successful ... was that the Poles had concentrated their men, equipment and cavalry. ... The Germans not only destroyed their planes, but they scientifically bombed all the runways in the first 48 hours so (the Poles) could not take off with the planes they did have on the ground. Hence, a plan such as I recommend for industrial centers in the United States is in keeping with what we are compelled to look forward to if might and force again gain the day. ..."

To shield the country's number one steelmaking center, Pittsburgh, Snyder proposed airports "at such places" as New Castle, Kittanning, Vanderbilt, Greensburg, Indiana, Latrobe, Somerset, Waynesburg, Washington and Uniontown. In addition, "we should have selected and mapped out level farm fields for emergencies. Arrangements should be made in advance with the farmers, just like we make with industry, that in case of a national emergency their fields would be used for landing purposes."

In addition to all of this, the Congressman proposed a "trans-continental road program." Designed to take shape over a period of eight years, this road building marathon would link the entire country. Highways would run north to south and east to west. Snyder promised to put a million men to work on the project, an economic stimulus impossible "under the present social, economic and industrial scheme." Besides, he declared, "our national defense web would be at least 20 percent stronger. ... We could cut our national defense bill at least $200,000,000 a year and still have as much, if not greater, national defense workability and strength."

A Second Homecoming: 1954 at Fort Necessity

Marshall's Man

As his authorized biographer, Forrest Pogue claimed he never worried about George Marshall's place in history.

"I feel the same way about Marshall that he did about himself," he said on one occasion. "He kept saying, 'History will take care of that.' And I would say, 'General, there are false impressions entering history that will take 200 years to eradicate and then it won't matter.'

"Well, he never accepted that, although he did agree there was no point allowing absolute distortions to remain."

In the same discussion with Pogue, in the summer of 1987 at his apartment near the Pentagon, he insisted that the recently-published final volume of his Marshall series had to do well. It was a time when Marshall looked increasingly irrelevant to the great events that remade the world between 1939, the year he became Army Chief of Staff, and 1951, the year Marshall retired from public service. To many historians of the period, Marshall looked like a front man. "Everyone knows he had nothing to do with the Marshall Plan," Pogue noted sarcastically.

Pogue was the author of four volumes on Marshall's life. The books were so authoritative and thorough researched that one Marshall scholar posited that as long as Pogue was around few others would even touch Marshall, which indeed was the case. Since Pogue's death in 1996, the number of Marshall retrospectives has blossomed.

The genesis of Pogue's books about the five-star general and Nobel Peace laureate was Marshall's refusal to pen his own memoirs. Following his retirement from public life offers poured into Leesburg, Virginia, where he and his second wife, Katherine, summered, and Pinehurst, North Carolina, their winter home. Once he was offered more than $100,000, a hefty sum in those days, for a series of magazine articles. Another time he greeted a book agent with the comment: "I know why you're here. I'm not writing my memoirs."

The reason for his refusal evidently stemmed from his World War I association with General John

"Black Jack" Pershing. A trusted aide to Pershing throughout the war, he helped the general execute his memoirs. That, and other works by generals who served both in World War I and the Spanish-American War, convinced Marshall that it was bad for the Army for erstwhile comrades to be pointing the finger of blame at one another. Besides, it was never in the General's nature to trumpet his own accomplishments. Marshall would let others speak for him.

That was the way things stood until September 1956, when he caved in to pressure from friends. Harry Truman and former aides, including Frank McCartney, who was working in Hollywood and would later produce *Patton* and *MacArthur,* and try and fail to produce a Marshall movie, persuaded Marshall to cooperate with a biographer.

Marshall did so on the condition that others choose who that might be and that profits from the sale of books would go not to himself or his family, but to the Marshall

Foundation founded in 1953 and headquartered in Lexington, Virginia.

In addition to chronicling the General's life, the biographer's duties would include the post of Foundation director. The person selected would thus confront a tremendous amount of work: interviewing Marshall, his friends and associates, and conducting the other research necessary for a multi-volume biography as well as starting up the Foundation with a minimum of staff.

Pogue hesitated. He had recently settled into a professorship at his alma mater, Murray State University in Murray, Kentucky, after turning down an offer from the University of Kentucky. The Marshall job looked like an endless series of administrative duties, with only sporadic episodes of writing. Pogue told the Foundation directors that he must get a firm commitment for one book. Otherwise, he would interview Marshall for a year, then leave. He got what he wanted.

He seemed perfect for the job. Holding a doctorate in diplomatic history and international relations, he had been an Army combat historian in World War II. (His good friend and fellow historian, Stephen Ambrose, quipped that Pogue "may well have been one of the best educated sergeants in the U.S. Army in World War II.") On D-Day, June 6, 1944, he had waited offshore in a landing craft hastily converted into a makeshift hospital and got the first interviews on the fighting in western Europe from wounded GIs. He followed the victorious American army into Germany. Later, he was selected to write the official U.S. Army history of the Allies' European high command. He spoke to all the main participants, including Eisenhower, although one of the few who turned down an interview request was Marshall. *The Supreme Command* was published in 1954 to critical and academic acclaim.

"Pogue by all odds was the most qualified person" to write the Marshall biography, noted Fred L. Hadsel, a former U.S. ambassador and a close friend of Pogue's going back to their time together in the late-thirties at Clark University in Worchester, Massachusetts, when Pogue was pursuing his doctorate and Hadsel was a graduate student.

Other scholars were considered. They included such luminaries as the distinguished diplomatic historian Samuel Bemis and military historians Hanson Baldwin and S.L.A. Marshall. McGeorge Bundy, later National Security Advisor to President Kennedy and president of the Ford Foundation, was also put under the microscope.

"They couldn't touch the bulk of those people," Pogue would recall. "They weren't paying that kind of money, and it required giving up positions to take the job, for it wasn't going to be a part-time job."

Katherine Marshall made clear the job was not going to be a snap. On one of Pogue's first visits to Pinehurst, she told him she did not favor the project, that Marshall's staff had unwisely talked him into it. She feared he was too tired and that it would be an imposition on him.

Several days into the interviewing, Marshall stopped the proceedings. "It's a bad day," Pogue recalled him saying. "I'm going to listen to the World Series."

At the start of the second session, Marshall abruptly handed Pogue a thick manuscript and told him to read it. The papers constituted a rough draft by an Army historian of the U.S. chiefs of staff during the war. Marshall had been sent the manuscript along with a series of questions to check for inaccuracies and omissions.

Pogue remembered Marshall saying, "'Now you ask me the questions.' He was intimating that I was suppose to cut out three-fourths of my own questions."

Pogue discovered that Marshall was an extremely private man. In his mid-70s, "he just didn't like people poking at him and asking him what he thought. I found that he responded well if you were fairly straightforward and somewhat formal. I was not there to be a 'hail-fellow-well-met', but he agreed to see me and gave me all the time I wanted and answer if he could."

Marshall's natural reserve, reinforced by years of Army discipline, melted only gradually, and never fully. On about their fifth encounter, Marshall greeted Pogue with the remark, "You look just like John Foster Dulles coming up the walk."

"Is that good?" Pogue asked, surprised at being compared to Marshall's Republican successor at the State Department.

"If a man's beating cancer," said Marshall, alluding to Dulles' fatal cancer then in remission, "you've got to respect a man's courage."

Pogue said that it helped if he mentioned a person both of them knew, such as General Omar Bradley. When they got to talking about some of the fighting in Europe where Pogue had served, Marshall would sometimes turn the tables and ask a question or two himself. Once, he responded to a Pogue inquiry about the "coddling" of infantry troops. Marshall's theory was that if the Army was going to ask men to fight and possibly die, it should at least try to provide some amenities. Whenever he could get ice cream or beer to the men, he did so. When GIs liberated one particular Belgium brewery, Marshall quickly cleared the way for production. He asked Pogue, "Did you get any of that beer?"

Still, the questioning went slowly. Marshall had various medical complications and he sometimes begged off answering questions because he wasn't feeling well. A breakthrough occurred when Pogue got hold of a tape recorder that could pick up the General's remarks from across a room. One of the methods Pogue used was to submit a list of questions. Over time, Marshall would respond.

"The old tape recorder bothered him," Pogue said. "He'd grab it and with the list of questions he'd crackle the paper and make the awfulest noise." With the mike not in front of him, Marshall could at least concentrate on the questions and Pogue was not longer stymied by a welter of extraneous sound.

Pogue believes Marshall may have suffered a slight stroke as early as 1957. Marshall experienced a kidney problem that required hospitalization in 1948 and, of course, he carried the burdens of the world for twelve grueling years - years of unusual strain and tension. He was ill with the flu, and later pneumonia, at about the time he accepted the Nobel Peace Prize in Stockholm in 1953. By the time the Pogue interviews started, he was largely worn out and occasionally stumbled.

"I found that if he didn't feel well or didn't have a very good night, the next day he'd say, 'Well, I'm not clear about that.' He had very common-sense answers. He'd say, 'It's not that I want to get out of doing this, but if later on people see that I say I don't remember, they'll wonder if anything you got is any good and that first part is all right.'"

The duo covered the war years, and Pogue got bits and parts of other episodes, including the post-war mission to China. The General did manage to talk extensively about his boyhood in Uniontown.

The Marshall tapes total forty hours. Little interviewing was done the last two years of Marshall's life. His death in October 1959, at the age of 78, from a stroke and its complications, ended Pogue's plans for a oral-history memoir.

"I had about one-hundred questions I thought were quite important which he hadn't answered," Pogue said. On his last visit with Marshall, the ailing General told him he was going off to Pinehurst for a rest. Afterward, he would resume speaking to the biographer. "But he never did."

(The Pogue interviews are collected under the title *George C. Marshall: Interviews and Reminiscences,* published in 1991 under the editorship of Larry Bland.)

Once or twice he rallied enough to converse with friends about the old days. These people would telephone Pogue with the good news. "They'd say, 'He told the most wonderful story about a Christmas party on post in 1906,'" Pogue related. "Then they'd advise me to go see him." Pogue declined, telling Marshall's friends they should grab a recorder and tape the story themselves. He told them, "I don't mean anything to him. I don't belong to that period. I'm just a questioner. If you're there, he's talking to an old buddy."

A meticulous researcher, Pogue conducted interviews with more than four hundred of Marshall's associates and friends, here and in Europe. He examined every edition of the Uniontown newspapers from just before Marshall's birth in December 1880 to 1902, when the young man was sworn into the Army by a town magistrate. His research was so exhaustive, one associate said, that "he intimidated everyone else into not writing about Marshall."

How good was George Marshall? By Pogue's lights, very good. The day the General left the Army as chief of staff in November 1945, he addressed a courtyard of Pentagon workers and President Truman. He was already looking ahead to the economic problems of Europe wrought by war, and his remarks foreshadowed the Marshall Plan speech at Harvard in 1948 by twenty months:

"Along with the great problem of maintaining the peace we must solve the problem of the pittance of food, of clothing and coal and homes. Neither of these problems can be solved alone. They are directly related to one another."

Marshall supported universal military training, believing, in Pogue's words, "that firmness required military strength. He warned constantly against slapping an opponent in the face while one was virtually disarmed. He deplored the use of harsh rhetoric, insisting that one must permit one's enemies room to maneuver."

Marshall was even hated by the right people. As Pogue makes abundantly clear, Senator Joe McCarthy, the Red-baiting Wisconsin Republican who terrorized Washington in the early and mid-fifties, tried his best to smear Marshall, but McCarthy and his henchmen failed miserably. Who could believe that Marshall was "steeped in falsehood" after all that he had done for his country?

(Just how big a problem the McCarthy virus was is illustrated by an exchange Pogue had with President Eisenhower about Marshall. Pogue knew Ike quite well. He occupied a Pentagon office adjacent to the general's while he was working on *The Supreme Command* and, as he explained, would sometimes pop in to ask the then Army Chief of Staff to clarify something or other. When Ike become president, Pogue presented him with a copy of the first volume of the Marshall biography. While at the White House, Pogue took the opportunity to quiz Ike about an episode involving McCarthy. During the 1952 presidential campaign, the candidate's staff released to the press the copy of a speech Ike was to give in Wisconsin containing a glowing endorsement of Marshall. With McCarthy sitting just yards away, Eisenhower omitted the reference on delivery. According to Pogue, Ike shrugged off the message that his actions conveyed - that despite everything Marshall had done for his career, Ike was more than ready to jettison his former boss on grounds of political expediency.

"Everyone knows how I feel about General Marshall," the president told Pogue. Decades passed and Pogue still had trouble with Eisenhower's answer.)

These many years later, Pogue's Marshall looks familiar: first in war, first in peace, an absolute rock of integrity. Marshall's reputation looks impregnable unless it's the case he failed to make for himself. He never bragged, preferring that credit goes to others. When for instance, he spoke of the Marshall Plan for the economic recovery of Europe after the war, he was apt to remind listeners that he merely gave the speech that launched the ship, a response that was highly misleading, as Pogue well knew, given Marshall's long and exhaustive cross-country speaking tour, beginning in Pittsburgh, to sale the American people on aid to war-ravaged Europe.

Besides, historical renown often rests on the shifting sands of public opinion and current events. When the second Pogue volume was published in the midst of the Vietnam War, Hanson Baldwin in *The New York Times* asked whether the infantry victories of World War II "have brought peace" or the illusion of peace. Perhaps the question can't be answered, Baldwin said, "but it must be raised, for Marshall was preeminently the champion of the ground soldier who believed the conquest and occupation of the enemy nation is the key question."

Forrest Pogue admired George Marshall above all other men. An exceedingly gracious individual, Pogue was a historian of penetrating insights. Wise in the ways of the world, he imparted all that he knew about Marshall, which was about all that anyone knew.

Each December for many years running, Pogue placed flowers on Marshall's grave, a charmingly plain outpost on the cusp of a steep hill in Arlingtion National Cemetery. Advancing age, cataracts, and difficulty in getting permission for his secretary to drive to the grave site caused him to discontinue the practice. "The flowers would be there for Christmas and his birthday" on December 31, Pogue said. "I understand you can make arrangements with a flower shop, but it's not the same. It was me taking the flowers."

Rally Around The Flag

Rose Brady at the train station in Connellsville

Mrs. Brady And The
Connellsville Canteen

It was a slow start, to be sure. Just one hundred and twenty-five sandwiches served along with just thirty six glasses of milk and one hundred cups of coffee. The first train was eastbound and arrived at 10:40 in the morning at the Baltimore and Ohio train station on Water Street. The Connellsville Canteen was open for business but it couldn't be called a success - not yet.

That didn't happen until the second day of operations. "Ladies," wrote a grateful serviceman en route to Washington, D.C., on April 11, 1944, at the same time that other U.S. soldiers were slugging their way up the Italian boot, in some of the toughest fighting of World War II, "we appreciate your coffee, sandwiches, cigarettes, and milk. We reached D.C. at 7:30 a.m. Our password is 'Remember Connellsville.'"

Corporal Hayward L. Kelley, going from Camp Haan, California, to Morgantown, West Virginia, where his brother Harwood was due from North

Carolina for a family reunion, told one of the Connellsville women volunteering at the Canteen that he had been riding coach for four days, and this respite - entirely unexpected - was just the thing a weary soldier needed. A Navy ensign, reaching for a cup of coffee, declared "I haven't been treated this nicely since I left Sardinia where I was treated so well by the Red Cross." The seaman ate three ham salad sandwiches and drank two cups of coffee.

On that second day more than thirteen hundred sandwiches and five hundred and sixty cups of coffee were handed out. It was only a warm-up. For two years starting in April 1944, the Connellsville Canteen would serve better than half-a-million sandwiches and amounts equal to that in "java", doughnuts (28,270 dozen), cigarettes (100,876 cartons), milk (28,309 quarts), and assorted other items including eggs, oranges, apples, soft drinks, and magazines.

One city official, during the Canteen's first anniversary, called the Canteen "a little enterprise all its own." It wasn't so little at that. The women, under the chairmanship of Rose Brady, raised nearly $50,000 during the emergency of war to keep the operation going. They arranged tag days, picnics, bake sales, and community events like the two performances of the play *Papa Is All* staged by the young people of Dunbar Township and directed by Dunbar High School drama coach Howard Smith.

And when cash was short, Mrs. Brady and her band of volunteers turned to merchants like Jim Shields, whose Connellsville A&P grocery store was "up the tracks" from the Canteen, for donations.

Twenty four hours a day, three hundred and sixty-five days a year, the Canteen was primed for action; every train - either a regular passenger train or a "special" troop train - was greeted with food and refreshments for the service men and women on board.

The numbers were prodigious. A troop train alone might contain as many as five hundred weary, famished GIs. During the thirty days between January 1 and February 1, 1945, for example, the women of the Connellsville Canteen served twenty nine thousand two-hundred-and-eighty-three sandwiches. On March 29, 1946, nearly a year after the war ended in Europe, the volunteers handed out two hundred and sixty-seven cups of coffee and one hundred and twenty-six doughnuts.

This generosity warmed many hearts, touched many lives. Writing from Italy in September 1944, one American soldier noted: "The (train) coaches, uncomfortable as they were, had no water and our rations were gone. Suddenly, one GI shouted loudly: 'Don't worry, fellas, we'll soon be in Connellsville. Then we'll get some real hospitality.' ... (At the) Connellsville railroad station, whether day or night, rain or shine, there always was hospitality."

Five hundred women volunteers toiled at the Canteen, blazing their way into local lore. Mayor Abe I. Daniels, speaking in April 1945, as victory over Nazi Germany rapidly neared, declared: "We have every reason to believe that no local project has brought Connellsville such a flood of fine compliments." The "Friendly City", the mayor said, was friendlier by far, "all because of the work of the women of the Canteen."

When Japanese bombs fell on Pearl Harbor in late 1941, they ignited not just the Pacific fleet; they transformed the nation. A divided people before the attack, Americans suddenly confronted a worldwide conflagration with vast military, political, and moral dimensions. Not since the Civil War had the nation been so imperiled. Germany, under Adolf Hitler, was fierce and menacing, the conqueror of Europe from the English Channel to deep inside the Soviet Union. Japan controlled most of the Pacific and Asia. And now these two nations had turned their might on America. If Americans felt secure separated by vast oceans from the troubled lands, east and west, Pearl Harbor shocked them into an awful realization.

By the winter and spring of 1944, when planning for the Connellsville Canteen was underway, prospects had brightened. The Allies (principally the United States, Great Britain and the Soviet Union) were punishing the Germans in Europe while in the Pacific and the Far East the United States was slowly but steadily stemming the Japanese tide.

But as national leaders were anxious to point out, the war was hardly won, and tough and costly fighting was ahead. Most Americans seemed to understand. In a sense, the war, although costly, was not yet the "American" operation it was destined to become. Full engagement would not arrive until the cross-Channel invasion of Europe in June 1944. With Allied soldiers streaming over the beaches of Normandy, an editorial in the Connellsville *Courier* cried out, "It's our war now!"

And it was.

Still, there was plenty for Americans to do and worry about in the winter and spring of 1944. There were victory gardens to plant ("Here are the reasons Victory Gardens must grow more in 1944," went one newspaper ad, the work of government public relations, "...10 million men in the service, 60 fighting fronts, huge civilian demand, needs of our Allies ..."), ration books to purchase, paper and tin to collect, planes to watch for, air raid warnings to heed, blood to donate ("1,070 pints of blood donated last week"), and bandages to wrap. Of course, there was the draft, a three-headed monstrosity run from Washington but implemented through state and local draft boards. Fayette County Draft Board No. 1 sat in Connellsville.

In the spring of 1944 Selective Service, as usual, was in a state of uncertainty; and citizens could hardly be blamed if they asked themselves, "Do the people running this shooting match know what they're doing?"

Naturally, the draft was necessary. Although there is truth in the World War II image of millions of able-bodied (and sometimes not so able-bodied) men volunteering, millions more did no such thing. Their reluctance was understandable, given the uncertainties of military service and the vagaries of life in general.

Because of the immense scale of the conflict, every personal plan was subject to change. Millions of men were learning that neither a civilian occupational deferment nor an age deferment nor a college deferment lasted forever. In early March, under pressure from the Army which was actually two hundred and eighteen thousand men *under strength*, the state director of Selective Service, Richard K. Mellon of Pittsburgh, let the ax fall; he directed local draft boards to begin the reclassification of men in critical occupations, including steelmaking and mining. Draft boards were told to "cut to the bone," sparing only those whose jobs were "vital" to the war effort. The directive also reshuffled the cards according to age. Now, a reasonable healthy thirty-eight-year-old could find himself hauled off to boot camp. Right away, six hundred Connellsville area men became draft-eligible for the first time.

Instead of rapid action, however, the men were left to twist in the wind. Washington was bogged down in detail and controversy. For one thing, the military faced a public relations disaster relative to its older inductees. As one of the higher-ups in the Pentagon, General Miller G. White, assistant chief of staff for personnel, put it: "The war morale of the nation" was at stake, given the fact that "public feeling is offended by the sight of numerous young men in civilian pursuits, while older and less fit men are" drafted.

As most everyone recognized, older men were not as eager to fight nor were they in the kind of shape to fight that younger men were, and the Army, by March 1944, was losing the competition to enlist young men - losing to the Navy and to the Marine Corps. The age of the average Army inductee was twenty-five compared to an average Naval enlistment of 23.6 years and 22.1 years for the Marines. Meanwhile, most eighteen-year-olds were choosing the Navy or the Marines. "All of the armed forces recognize how important it is to have hardened young men in their combat forces," Chief of Staff General George C. Marshall noted.

In addition, the civilian managers of the American economy were once again screaming their bloody heads off. The struggle for the last ounce of available manpower had been going on since at least Pearl Harbor, and it was still raging. The result was not a happy one. The men of Connellsville - men everywhere - and their families, were placed in quite an uncomfortable situation. "Groping through a quagmire of conflicting and ever-changing regulations" (as the *Courier* put it), men twenty-six to thirty-eight were packing one day and unpacking the next. They resembled, if anything, puppets on a string: up one minute, down the next. If they were to be drafted, they had the details of their lives to look after: businesses and bank accounts to close or transfer, wives and children to relocate; everyone had to have time to say goodbye. And if they were not going to be drafted ... well, the uncertainty was nerve-racking.

Then April 1944 brought a rash of inductions: forty four on April 12; forty five on April 19; forty three on April 20. The April 20 leaving was typical. The inductees, all from the Connellsville-Dunbar area, were ordered to report at 6:30 in the morning to the B&O train station. Their immediate destination was Greensburg, to be sworn in.

The men were leaving civilian life for the uncertainties of military service. The most significant of these uncertainties stood out like Betty Grable's legs, or more exactly, like a pistol pointed to the head: within weeks these erstwhile civilians could be fighting and dying. It was a sobering thought - for the men, for their families, for their friends, for the town.

Reading the local newspaper was like poking around in a house of horrors. Daily came reports that someone's brother, someone's son, someone's husband was captured by the enemy, was missing in action, or was dead in combat.

As the newspaper reports and the draft made clear, the war was far from over. And though Connellsville was hardly alone in this realization, the Canteen, in its peculiar shape and form, was the city's alone. As WAC Sergeant Virginia Smith, assigned to the Army Air Force Headquarters at Bolling Field, Washington, D.C., wrote in a letter of thanks to the Canteen, after eighteen months in the service and having traveled "most of the country east of the Mississippi," from what she could see Connellsville was different inasmuch as "yours is the only town of any size where the citizens have been so doubly considerate.

"So many places (have) canteens near the station but we are afraid to leave the train to go look for it. ... As much as the food and the thoughts ... we particularly appreciate the smiles and cheerful words."

It would be easy to assume, given the romanticized notions of World War II, that there was something inevitable about the Canteen; that Rose Brady, its creator and founder, had a star fixed in the heavens. In truth, nothing was preordained. Some distinctive mix of ambition, patriotism, opportunity, and personally felt obligation called the Canteen into being.

Rose Brady loved Notre Dame football. Fifty years after the fact, her daughters could still recall both the degree of enthusiasm and dread she brought to the games. Saturday afternoons in the fall Rose's special place was close to the family radio set. She tried to sit still; she never quite managed. If the Irish were losing it was next to impossible. Hopping up from her chair, she paced the floor, wringing her hands as she did so. It didn't matter whether Connellsville's Johnny Lujack, Notre Dame's All-American quarterback, was on the field or not. It only mattered that the Irish were playing.

Rose Brady had several passions. She took great pride in the tilt of her custom-made hats. Saturdays when Notre Dame wasn't playing it was her habit to leave home early in the morning to confer with Agnes Noonan, hatmaker. To her daughters, one of whom was always present, these discussions seemed to go on forever.

Rose also adored antique furniture. John Brady,

husband, insurance man and county prothonotary, was accustomed to regaling friends with the story of the morning he spied an especially sad-looking chair angled precariously on the rear of a truck. He said to himself, "I wonder what those people are going to do with *that*?" In the evening he discovered: the chair was his - thanks to his wife.

Still in all, John had to admit Rose knew what she was doing. The Brady residence at 403 E. Greene St., with its high beams and polished wood finish, was perfect for the furniture she collected. A rosewood table Rose had liberated from a heaping pile of throwaways dominated one room, an antique love seat another. Everything matched.

In addition to Rose and John, the Brady family consisted of sons John and Edward and daughters Ann, Rosemarie, Helene and Barbara (daughter Susan, adopted, arrived after the war). The household was informal and fun, with an undertone of seriousness. The family was fond of gathering around the radio Sunday evenings at seven to listen to comedian Jack Benny. Normally, they were settling in after a hearty meal, quite often potato dumplings which Mrs. Brady had spent the day preparing. She made all the family bread, too, even during the war years when she was otherwise occupied.

The children, naturally, were expected to pitch in at home. There were curtains to take down and clean, clothes to launder (and hang out to dry), ironing to look after, and a whole house, thirteen rooms in all, to dust and vacuum. All of this work was somehow made tolerable for the children by Mrs. Brady's knowing delegation of responsibility, and by the fact that she toiled longer and harder than the rest. Rose seemed to work all the time - at something.

Early in the war she entered the volunteer nurse program at the Connellsville State Hospital, and was soon a Red Cross nursing leader. Not only did she work hard (nine hundred and fifty volunteer nursing hours by the end of the war); she was in demand as a speaker and instructor. In October 1943, Rose paid a visit to the Mt. Pleasant Red Cross Blood Bank where, according to the unit chairwoman Jennie Madden, Mrs. Brady spent a considerable amount of time rendering "invaluable assistance."

Politics also engaged Rose. The Bradys were Democrats, and goings on at the courthouse were often the chief topic of conversation at evening meals. The fact that John had served as county prothonotary since 1928 gave the Bradys a front row seat at the ascent of the Democratic party and Franklin Roosevelt. In January 1937, John and Rose and daughter Ann attended FDR's second inaugural in a cold damp Washington rain. By then, Rose was a state committeewoman.

She was a celebrity - assured, successful, and mentioned often in the newspaper. During the war, West Penn Power sent a cameraman out to East Green Street to photograph Rose and the girls enjoying a new lineup of electrical gear, including a stove and a refrigerator. The Bradys were the stars of a local advertising campaign.

There was all of this plus private moments with John. Husband and wife traveled often, mostly as a result of John's prominence as a Rotarian. One fabulously romantic journey (or so it seemed to Helene and Ann) involved a train excursion to Pike's Peak in faraway Colorado.

In some sense, Rose Brady was ahead of her time, although there was the example of Eleanor

Roosevelt. Like the First Lady, Rose believed in a public accounting of oneself. It was her practice to stand at the kitchen window in order to watch her daughters head off to school in the morning; since they were unusually tall girls for their ages and prone to slouch, she would gesture for them to walk with their shoulders back. Her message was to be proud and strong, never give in or give up. Confront the world.

If Rose was ever torn between her public and private roles, and vexed as to how to reconcile the two, it was not generally known. Still, some hint of an underlying conflict exists in the letter she received from her priest-brother, Father Frances Bailey. Posted September 1938, the letter alludes to the fact that Rose was recovering from an emotional wound inflicted by friends, although no particular episode is mentioned. The sense is that of a wife and a mother searching for hitherto unexplored ground to occupy.

   "Before God and the world," Frank advises, "it's John and you alone for your own happiness and for the children. Bought friends are worth only what you pay for them and when you cease paying they turn on you. If you fail in your duty, they are the first to turn the finger of scorn at you and to laugh at you. ... Being conscientious about your duty as wife and mother may not bring you praise or adulation, but later on no one can say you neglected your duty."

No one could ever accuse Rose Brady of doing that. She was steadfast, and so was her family. When the time came to organize the Canteen, John Brady placed no obstacles in his wife's path, her children voiced no complaints.

As it was, she spent countless hours getting the Canteen up and running, and then worked hard for its success.

The idea for the Canteen was hatched by Mrs. Brady and Father Frances over coffee in the family kitchen. It must have taken some of its inspiration from the canteens organized in other towns and cities, including the famous Hollywood and New York City canteens. Later, Rose gathered together a quartet of prominent Connellsville men: former mayor Ira Younkin, newspaper publisher

James Driscoll, businessman and civic leader C.I. Sterbutzel, and Major Bryant of the Salvation Army. Mrs. Brady invited the men to the Brady's yellow brick house on East Green Street. And afterward, the *Courier* reported, "The above people pledged their full cooperation (to the Canteen) in every way."

These were the essentials: the Canteen would provide light food and refreshments to every service man and woman passing through town. The Canteen would be installed in the former Boyts Porter foundry on Water Street across from the Baltimore & Ohio Railway station.

The industrial setting, if not ideal, was at least convenient. The building would be redone inside: fixed up with a stove and refrigerator in a new kitchen, lounging chairs and couches in a reception area, and cots and day-beds for sleepy soldiers and sailors staying the night.

It was a foregone conclusion that the women of the town would operate the Canteen, with women from each of the city's seven wards responsible for a day of the week, and each day, as well as each shift, would have a woman in charge, an overall organizer and manager.

There were rules. Volunteers were to wear, when appropriate, hair nets and be courteous but not pushy about the food. They were told to let the men and woman in uniform cream their own coffee. They were to pay extra attention to hospital trains. They were to feed the policemen who patrolled the area and to record all telephone calls. They were to take no money.

The woman were cautioned about "spying or prying", and no tales were to be told, since the Canteen "usually (could) not be recognized after one was repeated." Later, new volunteers were told, "There never have been any serious mistakes. Try and quiet any gossip."

With 500 volunteers and thousands of trains to meet, some things were bound to go wrong. However, there were never any public reprimands or private scolding, at least none have come to light. On the whole, things were harmonious. Some of the women, it is true, groused about not being appreciated by the men in uniform, but these were momentary complaints.

What accounted for this unusual display of unity and common purpose? Simply, there was so much to do and everything, even the little things, seemed important. In the middle of March 1944, for instance, Mrs. Brady, in her role as chair of the Connellsville Citizens Service Corps, reminded city residents to be sure to pile their paper bundles on the curb in front of their homes for the monthly paper collection; and the *Courier* made the point that burning even one sheet of paper was "actually lending aid to the enemy" since used paper was badly needed for manufacturing and industrial purposes.

William Bergin may or may not have been, as the newspaper proclaimed, "Connellsville's first war hero." And yet, while home on leave in March 1944, he was telling some pretty hair raising stories. Bergin had been at Pearl Harbor when the Japanese blasted their way through the place, and he had been at the battle of Midway when the Japanese had gotten their first good licking. At Midway, he said, he had the distinct pleasure of knocking two Jap Zeroes from the air, then got knocked from the air himself. For his heroics,

Bergin was awarded the Distinguished Flying Cross.

As a member of a dive bomb squadron, machine-gunner Bergin was in on the initial U.S. counterattack on the Marshall Islands; he had been onboard the aircraft carrier *Enterprise* when General Jimmy Doolittle and his intrepid crew took off on their daring raid on Tokyo; he had been at Guadalcanal. In fact, Bergin said, he had been at "all the places where the Americans were defeating the Japs."

And he was looking forward to more. Speaking from his parents' residence at rear 210 E. Cedar St., Bergin told a reporter, in language that sounds borrowed from Pentagon public relations: "America is demonstrating its might. The big push will continue until the Japs are blasted out of Japan. It's my hope to be part of the outfit that goes in to put the finishing touches on the Nips. It's going to be a tough job."

Nor was this all. To his neighbors and friends in town, Bergin said "the biggest thing" for them was to keep up war production and to "steer clear of absenteeism" at work.

"If we do our bit we'll get this thing over with

much sooner than it may seem," Bergin continued, sounding less like a fighting man and more and more like a PR man's dream of a client, "but everyone has a share of the responsibility. If you're at home, dig in on the production line, get behind all the war bond drives.

"If you do your bit, you won't be bothered by a conscience when the shooting ends and the boys start coming home."

Bergin's was one of many names filtering across the pages of the newspaper in the spring of 1944. Shortly after the Allies laid siege to the Catholic monastery at Cassino, Italy, word appeared in print of the death of Army Private Donald Carl McElhenny, nineteen, of Connellsville. When his father, Frank, was informed on March 5, the news cut him to the quick. Surely, an error had been made. Frank was certain Donald was alive. But there was no mistake. Donald had been so young, and so eager to enlist. The previous spring, instead of sticking around for his high school diploma, Donald had gotten on a train bound for Greensburg to take the oath. He couldn't wait to serve his country.

Army Private Robert A. "Bobby" Burns died, also in Italy. Nineteen and a city native, Burns had resided with his parents at 404 Johnson Ave., a wood-frame two story on a corner lot. Young Bobby had worked at the West Penn garage before heading off to basic training in March of 1943. Which meant in little more than a year he had gone from small town boy to fighting soldier to corpse.

It was a miserable war all right, and some very good men were falling. Bill Malomaka had worked at Anchor Hocking before the Army drafted him well into his 30s. Now he had perished in Italy, at thirty-five. Joseph Natale was gone too, leaving behind a sister and three brothers and his mother, who last heard from her son in a letter posted from Anzio beachhead, where the Allies were bogged down and bloodied, trying for a breakthrough to Rome, thirty three miles to the north.

The fate of other soldiers and sailors and airmen and Marines was anyone's guess, though they weren't dead. Not yet anyway. Sergeant D.J.

Bergin, Bill Bergin's brother and one of four Bergin brothers in the service, had been reported missing as long ago as September 1943; now he was known to be a prisoner of war held by the Germans.

Wally Schroyer was first reported missing in February 1944; in April his family and friends in Connellsville found out the truth: Wally was in a German POW camp. Though bleak (and bleaker yet if the family had known the extent of his injuries), this latest information was surely a relief to Phyllis Schroyer, Wally's mother, at 110 Trader Avenue. Wally was a young man of some prominence in the community. A football star for the high school Cokers, he had enrolled at Penn State, where he was expected to play brilliantly. Instead, following his freshman year in May 1943, he had joined the Army, and now this.

Uncertainty for the Schroyers was over; for the Albine family of North Third Street, it was only just beginning. Army Staff Sergeant Robert L. "Bob" Albine went down in his B-24 Liberator bomber over Germany on February 20, 1944, and still there was no word of his whereabouts or condition.

It is barely imaginable the pain such episodes caused families, waiting and wondering at home. How much comfort could the Kimbles of Connellsville take in the knowledge that Lieutenant Charles R. Kimble was even then arriving "safely' in the South Pacific? And what dreadful foreboding crossed the minds of the mothers and fathers whose sons had signed up for Aviation Cadet training at the high school on Wednesday evenings? Seventeen boys were in the class, all from Connellsville.

One did not know whether to swell with pride or recoil in fear after hearing of the experience of Army Lieutenant Edgar S. Wood. In early March 1944, Lieutenant Wood wrote his father, J.C. Wood, of Connellsville. The lieutenant was in an Army hospital recovering from wounds of the leg suffered in Italy. He was doing nicely. He told his family the crutches he had been using were no longer necessary and he was able to walk the hospital grounds unaided. As for the Germans and the experience of combat, Lieutenant Wood wrote: "I led my platoon into battle. We moved forward and were face to face ... (though) we couldn't see them I had the effects of them being near."

"It was a winter of gross discontent," writes novelist James Jones, "in Italy as well as in the Pacific. More and more, for everybody, the war was becoming a permanent way of life, a condition that would just go on and on and on." Now, in the spring, from Washington, General Marshall wrote General Eisenhower, in London as the newly appointed Supreme Allied Commander: "Under present circumstances I see no great purpose to be achieved in Italy, aside from maintaining pressure on the enemy to prevent the transfer of forces to your front."

But what the high commanders said to one another in private was immaterial to the men being commanded. The wheel of fortune continued to spin and where it stopped nobody could be sure. Army Sergeant Angelo Vitale, missing since November 10, 1943, in Italy, was now firmly reported to be a prisoner of war. Sergeant Charles W. White was not a prisoner, was not even missing, it turns out. He wired his wife, Audith, in Connellsville (she was living with her parents, Mr. and Mrs. W. H. Pierce, "for the duration of the war"), that he was "safe and well" and was still flying, a gunner aboard an Eighth Army B-24 bomber.

What fate would befall the men, young and old, still awaiting enlistment? Husbands and fathers like Robert L. Ritenour, Charles R. Lilley, Harold E. King, Homer R. Leighty and Lewis Shipley, all registered with Fayette County Draft Board No. 1 in Connellsville and, as heads of unusually large families, until now excused from the draft. (Ritenour had the largest brood, eight children.) Clearly, sacrifice was called for.

What was a woman to do? An uncommonly large number - five hundred by the end of its two year run - chose service at the Connellsville Canteen. The women of Connellsville (and of Dunbar, Mt. Pleasant, Vanderbilt and elsewhere, even faraway Meyersdale in Somerset County) responded to Rose Brady's appeal for volunteers with something close to zeal.

The Canteen wasn't the only game in town

either. With the men away, suddenly there was plenty for a woman to do. Defense plants and the government were promoting almost daily in the *Courier*. "Do your part in the war," read one ad for the local Anchor Hocking glass plant. "Come out and work on a job that pays well, steady work (in) pleasant surroundings and working conditions."

Out-of-town jobs were available, too. "Good war jobs for Girls and Women," trumpeted the Armstrong Cork Co. of Lancaster, Pennsylvania. Workers could earn "real wartime pay making aircraft parts, magnesium bombs, bomb racks and shells (no explosives handled)."

The ads were hard to miss, often taking up three columns or more in the *Courier*. There was a urgency about them:

Wanted

Women   At Once   Girls
Light factory work in an essential war industry

Acme Die & Machine Co.
Latrobe, Pa.
Co. representative will interview applicants from 9:30 a.m. to 4:30 p.m.
Monday - Wednesday - Thursday
U.S. Employment Service

A revolution was underway. The nation, faced with the emergency of war, was reweaving its industrial fabric. By 1944, U.S. plants were producing fifty percent more armaments than all the Axis nations combined. In fact, worker productivity was going through the roof. It took workers just seventeen days to construct a cargo ship; a bomber could be assembled in thirteen thousand work-hours, down from two hundred thousand at the start of the war.

Women were in the forefront of all this. In 1944, some three-and-a-half million women were working on assembly lines, alongside six million men. All told, six million women would join the labor force during the Second World War.

It was all rather extraordinary. Washington columnist Helen Essary, writing in the *Courier*, lauded the "New Women" of 1944 not as "grim, horny-handed females" but as a new breed: "so smart and so willing in the national win-the-war job."

The country was brimming with confidence - a "tremendous exuberance" of the spirit, observed C.L. Sulzberger, which "showed up in pride over the achievements of its soldiers, confidence in its ability to surmount unexpected problems, eagerness to tackle unfamiliar enterprises and an absolute lack of inhibition."

And yet ... for every essay extolling the "new" woman there was a "Hints of Beauty" column advising "the quiet, retiring young lady." For every government job promising the successful woman candidate a "position for the duration of the war" ("some may become permanent") and a promotion in eight months to $1,450 a year, there was a newspaper photograph showing to best effect the physical charms of an aspiring actress or beauty queen (or often someone of more ordinary attainments, for instance, "Pat Franks, a Red Cross worker from New York City ...")

Rita Smyth, twenty-one in the spring of 1944, was one woman who was betwixt and between. A Connellsville High School grad, Rita was working downtown at the Personal Finance Company and volunteering at the Canteen. Deciding to better herself, she took a Social Security Administration civil service test at the Post Office in Uniontown. Her goal was a job in Washington, D.C. ("Houses available," one ad assured. "Rent: $12 a week.") Rita passed the exam, but turned "chicken" when the time came to leave home.

Anastasia McCarthy, a Canteen worker (her mother, Nell McCarthy, was "troop train" chairwoman), was a busy saleswoman in the men's clothing department at Troutman's Department Store in Connellsville. In 1942, after passing a civil service examination, she had the chance to become a defense plant inspector in Alabama. But Nell McCarthy told her daughter: "There's no way you are going to Alabama. There's enough around here to keep you busy."

"The money was pretty good (in Alabama)," McCarthy recalled years later, "but my mother said 'look at what you'd spend.' She was right in a way."

Mothers and fathers worried about their daughters leaving home for a career faraway could take some comfort from the views expressed by Dr. A.A. Brill, a New York psychologist, to a wire service reporter in March 1944. Dr. Brill noted that the war was not, as generally supposed, altering the morals of a whole generation of young women and the "link" between delinquency and female infatuation with men in uniform was a figment of the imagination. In short, the doctor declared, girls who "go bad" would "be delinquent even without the war."

But change was in the air. Out in Columbus, Ohio, the Ohio State University humor rag, *Sundial*, was under attack by alumni scandalized by a picture of a partially clad co-ed in the magazine's most recent edition. The editor, a co-ed herself, was called a "disrespectful, brazen little hussy."

The war was churning the social pot. "The

National Defense Program believes it is necessary to train every available person" read an official pronouncement handed out by Rose Brady to prospective Red Cross nurse volunteers, all women.

"Total" war meant total mobilization, and no agency was more intent on utilizing women than the military. The Army's goal to replace combat-ready GIs with women in clerical and in some other non-combat jobs was running into formidable opposition, however. The first difficulty, according to Women Army Corps chief Oveta Culp Hobby, was the poor "attitude" of soldiers toward women in the military. The second was the "apathy" of unmarried women to even limited military service. The Army commissioned a Gallup poll and found that sixty percent of single women thought their present occupations were more important than service in the military. Adding to the Army's problems (according to the poll) was the fact that a majority of women took one look at the drab WAC uniforms and declared them dreadful.

Clearly, something was required to turn the situation to the military's advantage. Stepping up to help was General Marshall, who provided a statement for nationwide distribution. He pointed to the "urgent need for women ... to enable the military effort to go forward. ... As the Army sends more and more trained men to front line duty, we have to depend more and more upon women to take their places. ... Not only are there many jobs that women do as efficiently as men, but there are also jobs women do better than men."

Barring "urgent family obligations" that might keep a woman at home, Marshall urged women to do their duty and join the service.

As it was, some two hundred thousand women enlisted in the WACs, the Navy WAVES, the Coast Guard SPARS and the Women Marines during the war.

Louise Rulli of Sixth Street, Connellsville, was not one of these. A Saturday volunteer at the Canteen and an Anchor-Hocking employee, Louise wanted desperately to join the service. Many of her friends had the same idea. The military seemed like a "good opportunity to make something" of themselves.

Young and old alike volunteered at the Canteen

Only one of these friends, Madelyn King, actually signed up, however. Louise was thwarted by the same elemental force that put a screeching halt to Anastasia McCarthy: parental opposition. Louise didn't even presume to ask her parents whether she might enlist. She knew from the get-go that it was a no-go, and in that era most daughters heeded most parents, even those "grown up" and graduated from high school.

Many women did as Lavina Maricondi did. She stayed home, in Connellsville, to care for her four-year-old son and to watch over the family business, Maricondi's Dairy Bar, at the corner of Crawford Avenue and Fourth Street, while her husband, Lou, was off to war. Lou Maricondi had wanted to give up the dairy bar. Lavina wouldn't hear of it, though she didn't know a thing about the business, didn't even know how to cook. She told Lou: what in the world are you going to do for a living after the war if we give up the dairy bar? She assured him the business would survive his absence. Her mother would pitch in.

And that is exactly what happened. Lavina

Maricondi willed herself into the role of business owner and store manager, with help from her mother, Mary Rivosecchi. Together they became cook, clerk, bottle washer - and baby sitter.

"It made it a little bit hard," Lavina recalled, "but we got it done."

As one of Rose Brady's handpicked Ward chairs, Lavina spent Saturdays overseeing activities at the Canteen. Arriving at eight in the morning, Lavina would see that the customary ham salad sandwiches were prepared by her team of friends and neighbors from Ward 6. Working at the Canteen was therapeutic for Lavina. Though still quite young, she had been active for years at the Sons of Columbus auxiliary in Connellsville. What with the business and baby to care for, she hardly had time to spare, not even time to grow a Victory Garden. One activity she always found time for was prayer. Her heavenly petitions were not so much for her husband, who was in the stateside Army; instead, she asked God to make safe the path of her brother Joe, a veteran combatant in the spring of 1944.

It was best to keep busy. Otherwise, worry might get the best of a person.

Another, perhaps unspoken, spur to activity was remembrance of the Great Depression - the bread lines, the unemployment roll, the dole.

Anastasia McCarthy, who had graduated from Immaculate Conception High School in 1941, was a child of the Depression. Her father, Edward, a railroader, had been one of the lucky ones: he was never without work. Uncles and aunts and family friends were not so fortunate; for some, the 1930s were the darkest hour of their lives. "A lot of our friends were just trying to survive," Anastasia recollected.

During the war, she noted, "people managed better. There was enough around to keep *everyone* busy."

Working at Troutman's department store, Anastasia was busy all the time. "We did all kinds of things. We sold war bonds in addition to performing our regular duties."

"Regular duty" included looking out for Troutman's "steady" customers. When, despite wartime rationing, the men's clothing department received a fresh shipment of shirts and pants, Anastasia always put some aside for special customers. Besides demonstrating business sense, it saved time, for in addition to work, Anastasia was a Girl Scout troop den mother. Once a week she volunteered at the Canteen.

This sort of frantic activity was not unusual. Rita Smyth performed triple duty: at work, at the Canteen, and as a volunteer with the Women's Motor Corps. The Motor Corps, sometimes referred to as the Ambulance Corps or the Connellsville Civilian Defense Drivers Corps in the newspapers, was organized soon after the opening of the Canteen. Its purpose was to "give a lift" to local GIs stranded in town. Operating from midnight, following the final trolley of the day, until six in the morning, the Motor Corps was a godsend for a good many fighting men.

All of this activity put a premium on punctuality. Rita was typical: bolting from the office late on a Friday afternoon, she and her friend Evelyn Horan raced down Crawford Avenue and in a headlong rush crossed Arch Street, in order to make it to the Canteen in time to help make sandwiches for the first of that evening's trains, which usually arrived close to 7 p.m.

The Motor Corps pace was less feverish, but no less exacting. Veronica Bradley and Betty Pritts, Rita's Motor Corps "captains", organized the squad into military ranks, complete with lieutenants, sergeants, and privates. The women attended drills and learned to march (and suffered the cat-calls of gentlemen admirers whenever they appeared in the occasional parade).

It was odd in one sense that Rita ever got involved in the Motor Corps: She didn't drive; still volunteering seemed the thing to do. She was young and somewhat adventurous. Her friends Judy Rankin and Dakota Olinger also helped out, and besides, the Corps allowed Rita to don a uniform. (Rose Brady hadn't overlooked anything.) Blue with brass buttons and cap, the uniforms were stylish, but more important, it enabled Rita and her compatriots to be in step with the times.

Rita was proud to serve. She felt she was helping the war effort, like her two older siblings: brother Jimmy, a Colgate University man, who was a Marine, and sister Audrey, a nurse and a Navy WAVE, who was shipping out soon to China.

Sue Renze was Rita's Motor Corps partner. Reporting for duty a few minutes before midnight, the two women first checked at the Canteen for early arrivals. If there were none, they proceeded to Sue's car, parked under a lamp post on Water Street. Rita and Sue might fall asleep, but if a train whistle blew they were wide awake in seconds.

Now, if a serviceman from Connellsville arrived in town late at night, he most often walked home or called someone to pick him up. Most of those needing a ride lived in the country - far out into the country, Rita recalled. "They were farm boys mostly. On our journeys it was always very dark and frightening sometimes." If they got too far from Connellsville, Sue might turn to Rita and say, "I don't know where we are." Of course, if the soldier was awake he could help direct but often the soldier, sailor or Marine, groggy from a long train ride and the lateness of the hour, was sound asleep, dreaming, perhaps, of his welcome home. Almost inevitably under these circumstances Sue would want to turn back. She was always anxious about finding their way out of the back-roads maze they were in. Trying to be a calming influence, Rita would say, "Oh, we'll find our way back."

Sue, who reported to work at the Renze Tobacco factory on the northside of town promptly at seven each morning, may occasionally have lost her cool, but when push-came-to-shove, never her nerve. She realized the obligation she and Rita had to these men in uniform. Perhaps General Marshall's wife, Katherine, was not far off the mark, suggesting in January 1944 that women somehow personified the very meaning of this huge war. Speaking in New York City to a war bond rally, Mrs. Marshall said there were "thousands of intangible threads stretching across the water, each one reaching some woman back home. Whether you realize it or not, you women symbolize what (our servicemen) are fighting for - their homes, their families, and their country."

Certainly, the notion that the war was being fought for wives and girlfriends and homes and picket fences was part of the psychology of the times. In part, of course, it was true; few Americans could completely disregard the idea that if the Nazis and Adolf Hitler and the Japanese had their way, enemy fighters would storm the U.S. shore line.

President Roosevelt, in particular, was keen on pointing out the dangers. "The individual stake" Americans had in "the preservation of democratic life in America" was clear, the President concluded in a speech a full eleven months before Pearl Harbor.

By mid-point in the war, Franklin Roosevelt had returned to this point dozens of times, perhaps never more effectively than in February 1943. Summing up his chats with soldiers and sailors and Marines on the fighting fronts, the President noted each man he spoke to said the same thing: "I am fighting for my country. ...

"One will say he is fighting for the right to say what he pleases and to read and listen to what he likes. Another will say he is fighting because he never wants to see the Nazi swastika flying over the First Baptist Church on Elm Street. Another soldier will say he is fighting for the right to work and earn three square meals a day for himself and his folks. ... But all these answers really add up to one thing: every American fights for freedom.

Betty Friedan, who would help give birth to the feminist movement twenty or so years later, recalled that as the news from overseas worsened "women as well as men sought the comforting reality of home and children. ... We were all vulnerable, homesick, lonely, frightened." Annie Hurst observed that the women of America "are retrogressing into ... that thing called The Home."

The whole world was heartsick. Most of the popular songs were melancholy, blue. Even the up tempo *Don't Sit Under The Apple Tree (With Anyone Else But Me)* was a lament. The American heart ached.

Yearning swung from the sublime to the ridiculous. William Manchester notes that "the most famous ad of the war" was something called

"The Kid in Upper 4." It pictured a young soldier "lying awake in a Pullman berth remembering 'the taste of hamburgers and pop ... the feel of driving a roadster ... a dog named Shucks or Spot or Barnacle Bill.' There's a lump in his throat, and maybe a tear fills his eye. It doesn't matter, Kid. Nobody will see ... It's too dark."

The ad was shameless, but effective. There were millions of scared American boys being hauled cross-country to a fate and a destination they could only imagine. And there were millions of equally scared American girls. The result was a desire to do the things that would help win the war and hasten the return to home of these forlorn GIs. Dorothy Keagy, whose father Harry Keagy owned Keagy's Drug Store on South Pittsburgh Street in Connellsville, summed it up many years later. "You volunteered, you did something," she said.

Goodbyes had real meaning in those days, and no goodbye had quite the sorrowful and wistful quality as that bid at the hour of parting between a GI and the girl he loved, or thought he loved. These parting scenes vibrated with life, with longing and heartbreak - for, in truth, in some instances, these were final partings.

It was customary in Connellsville to gather at the B&O station at every leave-taking. Each departure involved at least a dozen or so men, and sometimes up to two dozen or more. The Molinaro Band would play tunes and the townsfolk would mill about, shuffling across the wooden planks of the train station to the landing outside, perhaps pausing to glance at the magazines and newspapers sold at the newsstand at the side of the building, or to gaze at the Youghiogheny River, as it made its way north. Mothers and fathers, brothers and sisters, sweethearts and wives would be on hand, along with friends. Rita Smyth was on hand more than once. In the midst of an embrace, she and a fellow were brought up short by her mother standing nearby. "Young man," Margaret Smyth cut in sharply, "do you do that often?"

Bobby Burns, a good friend of Rita's brother Jimmy, had left for the service on one such occasion. Bobby's death in Italy, just as the

Canteen was about to open, shook up the Smyth household. "Here was someone you knew personally, who ran around with your brother, and who was in your home," Rita recalled. Rita's beau would die, too, although he really wasn't her beau, only a desperately shy young fellow at the train station. It was the accumulated weight of it all - Bobby's death, the other deaths in combat, the other young men from town wounded or lost or captured - that made it all so sad. At the same time, it bolstered Rita's determination to serve in the Motor Pool and at the Canteen.

Not every Canteen volunteer had so heartfelt a rationale. Some simply needed something to do. Others volunteered because they were asked, or because a friend had already stepped forward. Sometimes the "friend" was a relative, and it is true that an uncommonly large number of sisters, as well as mothers and daughters, volunteered in tandem, walking or driving together to the Canteen - civilian women in service to their country. The Buttermore sisters were the most celebrated example. Eleanor, Margaret, Frances and Beatrice served on the same evening shift.

Sally Richter was a special case. Born in a house on Connellsville's Peach Street, she eventually moved with her husband and their growing family to Colonial No. 3, close to Grindstone in southwestern Fayette County. The family returned to Connellsville in the summer of 1943, following the death, in combat, of Jack Richter, Sally's son. Jack was killed May 29, 1943, in North Africa.

Before Jack left for overseas he spoke about just such an eventuality. He told his mother not to worry. His fate, he said, was in God's hands. Sally understood then, but not later. She could not live in the house in Grindstone with its memories of Jack. She could not bring Jack back; she could, and did, volunteer at the Canteen. It was an imperfect substitute, of course; but it sufficed for a time; It was busy-work; it was catharsis. In this war, everyone, or nearly everyone, had a job to do. The Canteen was Sally's.

That troop trains stopped in Connellsville was hardly shocking. Since before Civil War days Connellsville had been an important railroad juncture.

The surprise was the length of their stay: brief, never, by most estimates, more than ten or fifteen minutes. This placed a premium on fast action, coordination, teamwork. The first line of response was the phone-call alert system Rose Brady and the others had devised. The initial notification was passed from the station master to that day's Canteen chair. She, in turn, alerted several of her volunteers, and they in turn called others. Often there wasn't a lot of advance notice. The government never allowed troop train movements to be publicized. Even station masters were kept in the dark until the last possible moment. But the women always managed.

The battle plan went something like this: make the sandwiches, ready the doughnuts, sort the fruit, group the magazines, pour the coffee, wheel the food cart into place, place the sandwiches, the doughnuts, the magazines, the coffee on the food cart, lift the food cart over the tracks onto the landing, haul the cart around the train station, wheel left or right, and then get as rapidly as possible to an assigned spot beside the tracks. Wait. The train troop, if the station master was correct, would soon be along.

One Canteen rule was that the sandwiches and such were not to be taken onto the train by the volunteers. Instead, the two volunteers accompanying each cart handed the food and refreshments to an officer or enlisted man who had climbed from the train to the ground. Sometimes, if the hour was late and few hands were awake, the rations were lifted onto the train through an open window.

Troop trains caused the most excitement. Even otherwise unengaged townspeople showed up, once they heard a troop train was on its way. A regular passenger train with service personnel on board was far less hectic, although their more leisurely pace allowed time for mixing with GIs, who would get off to stretch their legs. Several times trains crowded with German or Italian POWs came through. The first time this happened Rose Brady had to think a moment. Then she ordered the prisoners fed. The POW trains were shrouded in mystery, their curtains drawn. No one looked in, no one looked out.

No one on board the trains suspected the tremendous amount of preparation that had gone on beforehand. It was meant to look effortless, although it wasn't. "Right now we are pressed for hours to get the Canteen duties performed," explained Ruth Kunkle, third in charge. "There have been so many donors, of either cash, food, or furniture, that it would require considerable time to write each a personal letter of thanks."

Although letters of thanks arrived frequently from appreciative GIs, among the workers and leaders there was the nagging suspicion that the Canteen was under-appreciated. The Connellsville *Courier* was taken to task, privately, by the volunteers, who muttered that the paper was not printing enough about the Canteen. Mrs. Brady penned a letter to *We The People*, a CBS radio program in New York City, and heard back from program official Ellen Robin: "I'm afraid at this time that we can't do a story about the Connellsville Canteen. We have so many canteen stories that we feel they are getting repetitious." Sometime later, Patsy Graham, at Rose's bidding, wrote CBS again.

"I'm sure your listeners would be interested in hearing Mrs. Brady tell her story on *We The People*," Patsy told Milo Bolton, the program's producer. With "500 women enrolled and on active duty" it was quite a tale to relate:

Once, "the women met twenty-two trains in twenty-four hours, serving sandwiches, coffee, milk, donuts and many hand-made delicacies, fruits, cigarettes and magazines. All served free," Graham noted. "There have been occasions when the women made and served one-thousand sandwiches for one troop train, and the equivalent in coffee, milk and donuts. There has never been an instance when even the worst weather ever kept the carts from going out, for there never was a train missed."

Mrs. Brady never got to tell the Canteen story for *We The People* or for any radio show whose listeners numbered in the millions. The Canteen remained a secret, except for the volunteers themselves and the townspeople, and the five hundred thousand soldiers, sailors, and Marines who were treated so well. The service men and women, in turn, told their families and friends, as well as their buddies in the service. Occasionally, an out-of-town civilian also took note. All in all, the Canteen was not entirely unheralded, or unappreciated.

Private John J. Boland passed through Connellsville twice during the war. The first time was at four in the afternoon, and though the weather was cold, there on the train station platform were the ladies of the Canteen, dutifully waiting with coffee and sandwiches. Private Boland was astounded. The United States was a great country, but these women - these "good ladies" - were quite special.

What Private Boland never expected was to be treated a second time. But he was, this time at 1:30 in the morning. Boland was "really amazed."

Groggy from sleep, Boland stumbled off the train and got into the coffee line behind a veteran of the fighting in North Africa and Italy.

Boland watched as the soldier stepped up in line and a volunteer explained that the women had been waiting outside such a long time for the train to arrive that the coffee had cooled some. It was not, the volunteer emphasized, the hot, steaming cup a

GI deserved. She was sorry.

The soldier looked at his coffee cup a long second and said, finally, in a reassuring way, "Lady, if it was stone cold, it would still be good." And later, climbing back on board the train, this same soldier turned and remarked to Boland with a voice filled with pride, "*These* are *our* people."

This expressed Boland's own sentiments exactly. The women of the Canteen proved "our inborn conviction (as Boland wrote) that This Land Is Worth Fighting For."

Sergeant Charles Smith Jr., felt the same way - sort of. Writing from Camp Gordon, Florida, the sergeant declared that between Florida and Pittsburgh, only "Connellsville mothers" brought the "USO to us - not we Army boys hunting the USO." "Your kind deeds," Sergeant Smith assured, "will not be passed off lightly nor forgotten."

The same went for Harold Goslen, who apologized for all the noise that came from the coaches the day, or night, his train passed through town. "We may seem rough characters," he said, "but after being in touch with the fine things in life so seldom, men among themselves naturally grow harsh."

The Canteen managed to lift everyone's spirits, Goslen continued. "It was the realization that there were people within reach of us who thought of us as people rather than just so much manpower."

"To the ladies of the Canteen on duty at the B&O station early Tuesday morning" began an anonymous soldier, who reached Chicago on September 11, 1944. "If I could only convey to you the general atmosphere of the car I was in both before we stopped and after, you would most certainly feel repaid."

"I have never experienced such wonderful courtesy," wrote another soldier. From St. Louis came: "The Canteen itself is not large but what's there is 'tops'." Major Duncan Owen wrote: "Last Tuesday, 12 Feb., I passed through your nice and hospitable town ... (I've) been on quite a few troop trains during my time in the service & never have I seen men in the service treated in such a hospitable manner."

Some servicemen believed the Canteen was

affiliated with the railroad. Sergeant Albert Almassey Jr., asked if someone at the station might arrange for an exchange of tickets, "one reading from Connellsville to Washington." Another soldier lost a wallet and wondered if it had been "turned in" yet.

The Canteen had its civilian correspondents, too. Connellsville native H.C. Haddock owned a restaurant in Hagerstown, Maryland, and sent along a check for $25 as "thanks" and as a way to encourage the Canteen's "unstinting" efforts. Haddock had bumped into a soldier who had traveled through Connellsville. Broke with "nothing to eat or drink," he confided to Haddock, "some ladies who appeared as angels gave me two sandwiches, three cups of coffee, and an orange."

Haddock had heard of similar tales. Everyone, he said, speaks "of the Canteen with the highest respect and gratitude."

From Windsor, Colorado, came a note from Mrs. Richard Casten, whose "soldier-husband" had "raved and raved" about the Canteen's "thoughtful hospitality" in his letters home.

Traveling north from Florida, Mrs. Casten's husband had discovered "other towns" charging GIs "outrageous prices," including "15c for ice cream cones, 75c a quart for ice cream (and) 15c for a Sunday paper." Soldier Casten and his buddies "thought your kindness was really wonderful." Having heard so much about the Canteen, Mrs. Casten said she felt "guilty" that she wasn't doing "more for the war effort." But she had two small children to look after and they kept her busy. "I do give piano lessons so perhaps that helps the younger generation," she confided hopefully.

It was a lonely, empty time for many, and some soldiers, writing the Canteen, were sick at heart. Private Martin D. Baker was on his way to Ft. Meade, Maryland, from Texas, and thence to Europe, when his troop train paused in Connellsville. It had been a long journey, and everyone on board was either tired or hungry, or both.

Private Baker was most appreciative of the food and refreshment, and of the kind hospitality of the Canteen volunteers. He had always believed that women were "the sweetest people," and now, in Connellsville, he found it was so. He had a family

The war years were a lonely time for millions

of his own, he wrote, "a wife and two babies ... one of the sweetest families in the whole world." He thanked "each and everyone" of the volunteers, and noted that he felt he could "find comfort" and a welcome in Connellsville "at any time." He concluded: "I will let you hear from me after I go across."

Sergeant Howard P. Rankin, after noting the Connellsville Canteen was "the only 24-hour Canteen I've seen," declared: "All of us hope the day is not far off when you will be forced out of business and we will be able to pick up our lives where we left off."

Michael Frenchak actually wrote twice, both times from overseas. On July 9, 1944, briefly: "Maybe we'll meet again - Bless you all." On October 27, a little longer, "All of us remember such places as your Canteen. Thank you for being there when a tired GI needs a hand. Thank you people of Connellsville."

Thank you, indeed.

Until the appearance of the 1945 Connellsville City

Directory, Rose Brady's name was never listed separate and distinct from her husband's name. In the 1945 Directory, that changed. The Brady family now included: "Rose, Mrs. - general chairman Connellsville Canteen."

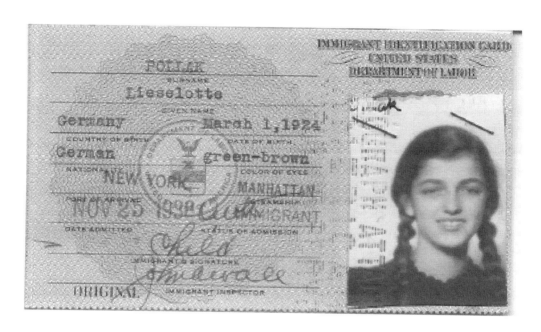

Lieselotte Pollak: U.S. Immigration Card, Nov. 25, 1938

The Americanization of Lisa

Normally, the Austrian spring is exquisite. The spring of 1938 was different. During the second week of March the German army "liberated" Austria. The following day - March 13, 1938 - Austria was formally incorporated into the German Reich.

For Jewish residents of Vienna like Lieselotte Pollak and her mother Elsie, the coming of the Nazis was literally the beginning of the end. The teachers at Lieselotte's school began wearing Nazi armbands. Students suddenly became one thing or another: a loyal Nazi or a Jew.

On the broad Vienna thoroughfare where Elsie modeled coats in a fashionable shop two German soldiers entered the shops and ordered the Jewish merchants, shopkeeper, clerks and customers into the street.

Elsie went meekly along. She anticipated what was to come. It had happened before, on other streets, to other Jews. They would stand a while, vulnerable as sparrows with clipped wings, then be ordered into Army lorries and carried away. No one knew exactly where.

And although it didn't happened this time - this time the lorries never came and hundreds of men and women were ordered back inside - it could happen again, at any moment.

One afternoon Elsie heard a knock at her front door. When she answered she saw two SS men blocking out the sunlight from behind. They saluted "Heil Hitler!" and entered. They went from room to room looking ... for what? After searching for a long time, they finally took Elsie pocketbook and turned it upside down. A letter from her brother living in the United States fell out and, with it, a ten dollar bill.

Before the SS men turned to leave, they faced Elsie. "Get out of Austria," they said. "Get out, quickly."

Elsie had an opportunity to glimpse the source of these mad changes. Within days of the German annexation of Austria, Adolf Hitler paraded through Vienna. He was a native Austrian, and had lived in this city of grand style as a political vagabond and tramp artist some thirty years before. Now the Viennese lined the streets for miles and cheered wildly as the Fuhrer waved from his black Mercedes Benz convertible.

It was evident many thousands of Viennese looked to Hitler to ease their misery. Many were hungry. Elsie herself reported "many thousands sat in winter around the stove sharing nuts, and some of the nut shells would be thrown into the little stove to heat the room, and some would be kept for income, because with so many pounds of unshelled nuts (families) got so much money."

Hitler would change all of this, and much more. As Elsie later recalled, "One had to be there to get the feeling" of hatred toward Jews.

Now it was customary for Hitler to parade under perfect sunshine, and this day in Vienna was no exception. The throng lining the streets was enormous, all the more so because German soldiers, before Hitler's arrival, had ordered everyone out of the stores and apartments along the motorcade route. No one was permitted to linger behind, to stoop, or to stand behind the darkened panes of glass inside the shops.

Except Elsie, afraid and uncertain of "how Jewish" she looked, did stay behind. She spied Hitler through tiny slits in the shuttered windows.

At school, Lieselotte learned of the reaction of

a classmate's father, a Jewish banker, to these heartbreaking events. On the morning of the annexation, a clerk greeted him. "Mr. Grossman, have you heard? The Germans are marching into Austria." Grossman answered "good day" and walked out of the building. It was believed that he bought a train ticket and fled to Switzerland.

Life was suddenly dangerous, and uncertain. That summer Lieselotte's parents received permission for their daughter to visit her grandparents in Czechoslovakia, on the occasion of their fiftieth wedding anniversary. On the eve of her departure permission was rescinded. The closing of the German-Czech border followed.

Around the same time, Lieselotte's father, Ernest Abram, a Viennese newspaperman estranged from his wife, escorted his fourteen-year-old daughter to Gestapo headquarters in order to obtain documents allowing her to leave Austria for the United States. Years later Lieselotte recalled the strangely friendly greeting her father received from the Nazi officer in charge. "Hello, Ernest. ... What can we do for you?"

In early November 1938, the assassination in Paris of the German ambassador to France unleashed a reign of terror on Jews under Nazi control. The assailant had been a young Jewish man. The SS newspaper *Schwarz Corps* declared that Germany, using the "Jewish principle of an eye for an eye and a tooth for a tooth," intended to "take a thousand eyes and a thousand teeth."

The newspaper labeled German and Austrian Jews "hostages," and declared, "We shall use the Jewish hostages systematically no matter how shocking some people may find it."

The authorities revoked the right of Jews to live in their own homes and apartments, with the result that Jews were subject to immediate eviction. Jews were forbidden to own property in excess of $2,000.

Press reports speculated that as many as fifty thousand Jews were being detained. In Berlin, eight thousand Jews were rounded up in one day.

"Hitler had passed a Rubicon," the Nazi architect Albert Speer wrote years later, "... and had taken a step that irrevocably had changed the fate of his country."

At the White House, President Roosevelt told reporters that the American people were "deeply shocked" by events in Germany. "I myself could scarcely believe that such things could happen in 20th century civilization."

The Uniontown *Daily Herald* declared, "The newest Hitler program simply turns America's collective stomach," but cautioned that "it would be bad if Hitler should discover he could get concessions simply by tightening the thumbnails on the Jews. ... This protest against the savagery of the Germans is a reaffirmation of our faith in the American way of life."

A newspaper cartoonist drew a Nazi cap poised over a waning candle. The caption: "More light, more light."

It was no easy task fleeing the clutches of the German government. "The problems the Nazis put in front of everyone were horrendous," Elsie recalled.

Nazi paperwork and red tape could sabotage even the best-laid plans. A person had to satisfy a number of requirements Were all taxes paid? How much money was being taken? What about a criminal past? Immunizations? Was there insanity in the family? Most vexing of all, the Nazi placed a two week time limit on departures. If, after two weeks, one still hadn't left, the process must start again.

Equally troubling was finding a country to which to flee. Elsie's brothers and sisters had immigrated to the United States beginning in 1921. Elsie's brother, Oscar, living in Hartford, Connecticut, pledged in an affidavit to support his sister and niece until they could stand on their own feet - an absolute, ironclad requirement of U.S. law.

Yet the United States was hardly a cinch. A nationality-based quota system was in place. Elsie sought help at the American embassy in Vienna. She was told that if she wished to enter the United States with Lieselotte, both must apply under the Czech quota, smaller than Austria's and fraught with delays.

Lieselotte hardly relished the idea of leaving her

mother and traveling thousands of miles alone to the United States. She began to say as much to the embassy official when Elsie spoke up: Lieselotte would be able to leave at any time, and traveling under the terms of the Austria quota would not be a problem. Elsie later remembered her daughter "was the most unhappy child because she wanted to come with me. But I felt her safety was more important."

More worrisome, for Elsie, was the train ride from Vienna to Hamburg, and the Nazi requirement that her papers remain current.

The day before their departure, Elsie discovered Lieselotte's tax certificates were not in order. "I didn't know what to do," she recalled.

"My father took me down to the (ticket agent office) to turn the ticket in," Lieselotte remembered. And the clerk there said, 'Who is going to ask about these papers when she lands in New York? You go," the clerk told Lieselotte.

"The people on the ship told me that all the way from Hamburg to New York Lieselotte sat with a big towel and cried and cried and cried," Elsie remembered. "And she was sick. She was only fourteen and she didn't realize what I had done was more or less a sacrifice."

In Austria, meanwhile, civilization was unraveling. The Nazis arrested Lieselotte's father and sent him to a concentration camp. When Elsie returned to Vienna, she discovered she would not be living alone. Two SS men stood at her door; standing next to them were a man and a boy, Jews whose property had been seized. These two will stay with you, Elsie was told.

On board the ocean liner *President Harding*, Lieselotte was placed in the care of a family named Meyer.

"Most of the children (on the ship) had come with someone, though I do recall either a boy or a girl alone," Lieselotte said. "A lot of the men had shaved heads because their wives had gotten them out of the concentration camps. The first night there was a lot of cheering because there was white bread on the table."

Lieselotte knew very little about the United States. She knew she had uncles and aunts and cousins there.

As the ship approached the United States a winter storm came up. Inland, the storm was the worst on record for November. Starting Thursday afternoon, just as families were sitting down to Thanksgiving dinner, snow began to fall from Georgia to the New England states. The entire East Coast was soon blanketed.

Friday, November 25, 1938, was bitterly cold in New York City. Late in the afternoon, the sky partially cleared. Most of the passengers were below deck packing their bags when someone cried out, "You can see the Statue of Liberty."

"The sun was going down and it was windy," recalled Lieselotte, who ran to the top deck with the others, "but the sky was fairly clear, just ragged clouds being drive across the harbor, and (there was) the sinking sun and the lady in the harbor."

Afterward, Lieselotte and the other passengers descended the gangplank into waiting embraces. Standing watch for Lieselotte was Uncle Oscar, his wife and children. They took the train to Hartford. In the bosom of the family, Lieselotte remained frightened.

Elsie arrived in the United States sooner than she expected, on New Year's Eve 1938.

Elsie felt she had wings - "coming from a place where everyone seemed to be your enemy and here you were with a crowd of people with open arms, everybody eager to touch and to kiss and to hold you.

"That, you can't describe. I was young. I had my child. I was expecting a good life."

Several hours later, at approximately nine in the evening, Elsie, Lieselotte, and the rest of the family walked into Times Square. Thousands had already gathered for the celebration that would take place at midnight. "I had on a very pretty black coat and a little muff and inside of my muff I had my purse," Elsie recalled. "And here I am squeezed in like a herring. I couldn't move."

To wade through the crowd, Elsie lifted her arms over her head and followed her brother. They finally worked their way to a restaurant where Elsie was introduced to American pancakes. Outside on the street the celebration was just beginning.

Close to Thanksgiving of that year, two hundred and fifty-seven men and eighty women became American citizens during a ceremony at the Fayette County Courthouse. It was the largest swearing-in of its kind in county history.

The air was festive. And because each new citizens required two character witnesses, the courthouse was full. The hallway outside the courtroom of Judge Russell W. Carr resounded with laughter. One of the new citizens - a man from the village of Leith - told a reporter he had never been arrested, though he had been locked up for "safekeeping" on several occasions.

Another man, asked what citizenship meant to him, smiled and said, "Now I can vote and kill *rabbits.*" New citizen Catherine Hydak of Everson celebrated her birthday on this day. She was especially happy.

Naturally, not everyone was overjoyed. One man was required to pay a $250 fine for a 1923 misdemeanor before he was allowed to take the oath.

In time, Elsie and Lieselotte moved from Hartford, Connecticut, to Uniontown to live near another of

Elsie's brothers Julius Spitzler. Elsie remarried. Lieselotte, now called Lisa at the suggestion of a cousin, attended Uniontown High School, graduating fourth in the class of 1942, the same year mother and daughter became citizens.

At their citizenship hearing the judge asked Elsie's sister-in-law Opal Spitzler whether, in her opinion, Elsie would make an upstanding citizen. "I think so," Opal said.

"You only think so, you don't know? I have to excuse you as a witness because you don't know for sure."

Whereupon, Opal told the judge that Elsie would make a fine citizen.

Her senior year in high school Lisa wrote an essay about the country and World War II and patriotism. The essay found its way into the local newspapers.

"Today," Lisa wrote, "we are trying to keep the flame of liberty burning, trying to preserve the spirit of our ancestors, the ideals of the pioneers.

"(Our aim is) to keep the torch held high in the hand of the Lady in the Harbor, to retain our

Fourth of July fireworks, our ballot boxes, our institutions of learning, our football games and proms, our picnics and family circles. ... This is worth fighting for."

Of the millions of immigrants who had come before her to this country, Lisa wrote, "Onward and onward they marched, those pioneers of freedom and equality.

"After leaving the tyrannies of European rulers and shaken the dust of oppression from their shoes, those rugged men wanted to live their own lives and they were willing to fight for what they thought was just and right. Such was the spirit of our ancestors. Such was the way of our forefathers."

Lisa attended the Indiana State Teachers College, in Indiana, Pennsylvania. While there she received news of her father. He had managed to escape the clutches of the Nazis. He was living among the Jewish refugees in Shanghai, China. Though that city was occupied and ruled by the Japanese, he was safe. Over time, the family learned the fate of other relatives. Ernest's mother - Lisa's grandmother - and his sister, plus an aunt, uncle and two cousins died in the concentration camps.

It is now many years later and World War II is long over. Lisa's husband, Leonard Burger, talks about his wife. He believes Lisa's early years shaped her subsequent life, her marriage, and the raising of the couple's only child, a son named Jim. Leonard Burger noted that his wife "doesn't take freedom for granted."

Elsie opened a book of photographs from the twenties and thirties. Most of the photos show Lisa, small and skinny and smiling. There she is on the beach in summertime, with her mother in their Vienna apartment in winter, and so forth.

One photograph is especially striking. It was taken one May during a surprise snowstorm. It shows Lieselotte and a small Austrian boy in a public square. They are quite young, six or seven years old. They appear happy, they have been playing. They are framed in white.

"This is Otto," Elsie said. "His father was a railroad man. He was a very, very intelligent boy."

Was Otto Jewish?

No.

Yet he and Lisa were friends?

"Yes," Elsie said. "He and Lisa became very attached to each other."

This particular May was long before the coming of the Nazis, Elsie explained, and Vienna was still a beautiful city.

What happened to Otto? Elsie was asked.

"He was killed in the war," Elsie answered. Otto Kaltenhuber had been a soldier in the German army.

Soldiers and Neighbors

When America entered World War II, the whole nation took up the fight.

One out of every 10 Americans - 16 million men - was in uniform between 1941 and 1945.

Cities and towns and the countryside, all took to the battle station. Neighborhoods, too. Hilltop neighborhood in Greensburg was one of those that shouldered arms.

Shoehorned between Vine Street on the north and Bierer Street on the south, Hilltop consists of 16 often narrow streets. During the war, there were as many as 181 households in Hilltop; nearly half were Italian-American.

From these streets and homes, Hilltop contributed nearly 90 of its sons to the fighting.

John DePaul of Jeannette, a retired Pittsburgh business executive and local historian who has studied his old neighborhood, said he could not "but help think that Hilltop, because of the size of its families, gave more men to the war than just about any section of the city."

DePaul noted that 14 percent of Hilltop's World War II population wore the colors; 21 percent of Hilltop's Italian-American population was in uniform. "That ... figure is well above the national average - in fact, 84 percent higher."

Both of John's older brothers, Ozzie and Mario DePaul from Steck Street in Hilltop, were World War II soldiers. Mario was wounded, on February 19, 1945, three days past his 19th birthday; hit by shrapnel from a German 88mm shell, Mario spent a total of 18 months in the hospital recuperating from his injuries.

In the thirties and forties, Hilltop was home to a great many large families.

One example was the Salvatore family of 413 Margaret Street (all addresses are taken from a 1946 publication, *Service Album for Greater Greensburg*). Frank and Concetta Salvatore were parents to seven sons. Five of the boys were old enough to have experienced World War II first hand.

James, the oldest, spent the war years stateside while Anthony shipped off to the Pacific for the fighting at Guadalcanal; Thomas slugged it out at the Battle of the Bulge; Frank Jr. saw action on a PT boat; and Richard was a Navy swabbie.

"My dad hated the Germans and the Japanese," recalled Lou Salvatore, who, having been born in 1932, was not quite old enough for the war. "He called them brutto bastards - ugly bastards."

Lou's mom was "always a little sad" during those years. The war, he said, "took a toll" on his mother - the anxiety of having five sons in the service was just too much.

According to the World War II historian Thomas Childers, mother Salvatore's reaction was hardly unusual.

Defeating the Japanese and the Germans was imperative, Childers explained. No one denied that. But knowing the importance of the war and the need for sacrifice was small comfort to those who were left at home, those who were left behind to wait and to wonder.

"The war was a strain on all the mothers in the neighborhood," said Tony Testa, who was 18 when he was drafted by the Army in 1943. "I'm sure not a day didn't go by that they didn't worry about it."

Testa, whose residence on Truby Street is just doors away from his childhood home, said being drafted "made me wonder what I was getting into." His mother, Mary Ann, who spoke little English and read none (his parents were born in Italy), wept when she was told the news.

John DePaul recollected his mother's despair after getting word of her son Mario's brush with death.

John was alone at the family residence, his parents attending Lenten services at the nearby Our Lady of Grace Church, when a telegram - dreaded in those days - arrived from the War Department. John recalled his pulse quickening. He tore open the envelope and began to read.

"The Army got it wrong," John remembered. "They said Mario had been 'slightly' wounded. Well, his wounds were severe, but we didn't know that. So I kept repeating to my mother, 'He was *slightly* wounded.'"

Nothing could assuage Armelia DePaul's anguish.

The war years were like that - everyone was a little afraid.

There is the story that Mary Beth Weyant tells of her father, Pete Giron. "My father delivered telegrams for Western Union in Greensburg during World War II," Mary Beth said. Riding his bicycle, Pete, who was 15 or 16 at the time, ventured all over town, including into Hilltop. Delivering a telegram to a family with a son in the service, he made sure to pedal away extra fast in order not to hear the cries as the telegram was opened.

Still, "he was able to hear the screams in the distance," Mary Beth said.

Other times he might be asked to read the telegram to a soldier's loved ones. The country was much more "ethnic" then. Many Americans didn't know how to read English. Pete Giron always declined to do so for families who asked, explaining that company rules prohibited it.

"The fact is that the people who immigrated to the United Sates between 1900 and 1925 ... fell in love with this country," said John DePaul, whose mother and father were both born in the Old Country, but adapted pretty well to life in the United States. John's father, Carmine, was a newspaperman and publisher of *The Sentinel Press*, known to the Italians of Greensburg as *La Sentinella.*

For all of their patriotism, however, many Italian-Americans began the war under a cloud, a result of Italy's alliance with Nazi Germany and the natural pride many Italian-Americans felt in Italy's military conquests in the several years before the Japanese attack on Pearl Harbor.

In the earliest days of the war, scores of Americans of Italian heritage were jailed on the flimsiest of charges, a 2001 Congressional report found.

While John DePaul can't imagine anyone from Hilltop being under FBI surveillance, he remembers as a boy begging his parents not to speak Italian on the bus on the way downtown. He "didn't like the glances" the family got from the other passengers, he explained.

America's entry into the war dispelled any doubts about the loyalty of Italian-Americans to the United States. As the historian, John Morton Blum, has noted, the "confusion" that attended the summary detentions in the hours and days after December 7 pretty quickly gave way in Italian-American communities across the country to an embrace of American victory in the war, even if that meant sending troops to fight against the Italian army on Italian soil.

Hilltop was a world unto itself in those days. It has its own grocery store (DeBone's Market on Steck Street). Its own drug store (Hilltop Pharmacy on Tremont). Its own barber shop (Angelo's also on Tremont). Its own bar and restaurant (Felice's at the intersection of Highland and Bierer). And its own auto repair shop (Zappone's on Vince Street).

"Hilltop was alive with the sights, sounds, and aromas of the old country," John DePaul said. He recalled the fragrance of tomato sauce and meatballs, seasoned with garlic and fresh herbs, wafting out of homes on Sundays. And the aroma of the bread, baked in outdoors ovens, was "sensational," he said.

In addition to backyard gardens, Hilltop had its own World War II Victory Garden on land adjacent to 8th Ward School.

The neighborhood produced its own war heroes as well. Perhaps none gained greater renown than Frank L. "Hank" Spino of 408 Wood Street. As a 23-year-old (and one of eleven children), Hank became a B-17 bomber pilot. A slender 123 pounds, Spino was on his way to the east coast from Salina, Kansas, when he flew his Flying Fortress over Greensburg, managing, as he said, to "buzz the old Hilltop neighborhood."

Angelo Rose, growing up at 410 White Street, remembered "everybody was at the window" at school when Hank brought his plane in low and fast.

In an unpublished oral history for Saint Vincent College, Spino said "people still ... call it 'the day the chimneys shook.'"

In 1943, Hank and his crew were shot down over Germany. He spent the remainder of the war in a German POW camp.

Others also rendered outstanding service. Anthony "Tutta" Reno of Highland Avenue was part of an amphibious combat engineer team which waded ashore on Utah beach hours before the main Normandy landing on June 6, 1944. Neither Tutta nor Tony Testa talk much about the war years (although Tony delights in telling the story of leaving for the service. Piling into a car with fellow Hilltopper Frank DeFloria, off they sped to the Greensburg train station, where a troop train was waiting to whisk them away to parts unknown). Tony took part in the invasion of southern France in August 1944. Michael Germano was one of five Germano brothers with service in the war. As a member of the 1255th Combat Engineers, Germano fought at the Bulge and was in on the liberation of Luxembourg, Belgium.

Four Hilltop men died for their country.

John Damato of King Avenue was killed in France.

Tony Deverse of 519 Catherine Street was a tail gunner in the 22nd Bomber Squadron, 341st Bomber Group, when his plane was lost in March 1944 somewhere in the Pacific.

Jack Reamer of Highland Avenue died on December 18, 1945, in the crash of his airplane.

Jack is memorialized at the Manila American Cemetery in the Philippines.

Finally, Julian Poli of 436 Steck Street was injured in a pre-flight training accident. Hospitalized and then discharged from the service in June 1943, Julian died as a civilian, in Greensburg, on December 15, 1944.

None of this is to say that Hilltop was unique. Other neighborhoods sacrificed just as much. To take just one example, perhaps no street in greater Greensburg produced more soldiers than Poplar Street in South Greensburg.

And just to be clear, being Italian was not a prerequisite for service in World War II. There were the five Evans brothers. - Meade, George, Frank, Tom, and Michael. All saw action, including Tom, who won a Distinguished Service Cross for "a fierce exchange of fire" with a tank and other heroics against the German enemy in November 1944.

The Evans brothers hailed from Perry Street. That's in Hilltop.

The Future Is Now

And Welcome Home

In late September 1946, John McGill, a large, raw-boned ex-GI, and his wife, Kathryn, found themselves at the courthouse in Uniontown. Nine months after his return from service in World War II, McGill was about to take possession of 105 acres of farm land. Owing to his own ambition and drive and a loan from the United States Farm Security Administration and its Fayette County subsidiary, the Farm Ownership Committee, McGill was stepping out in the world.

At twenty-two, McGill was thrilled by the prospect of becoming a landowner, a farmer. The loan itself was generous, a forty-year term at three percent interest. The property in Franklin Township cost $4,400 and was sandwiched between Route 51 and the coal mining community of Smock. Including house and barn, the farm consisted of a series of steep ravines good for grazing, though some trees on the property would need to be cut and the vegetation trimmed. An experienced farmer, McGill saw that there was room for crops, including corn, on some relatively flat land separated from the house and barn by a winding country road. For sure, the place needed wired for electricity and a new water well was in order, but John could take care of these himself, and in a hurry. All in all, it seemed just the place for the growing McGill family, son John Jr. having been born while dad was off to war.

A ceremony was held at the courthouse. County commissioner Paul R. Seeman, county school superintendent Harry Brownfield and G. Emerson Work of the Farm Ownership Committee were on hand to hear McGill tell his wife, "Now the farm is ours." To the courthouse crowd, McGill expressed his thanks. "It will be good to work land that belongs to us," he said. "I want the leaders in this plan to know how much my wife and I appreciate what they have done to make this possible."

And afterward, in the newspapers, it was noted that the loan to the McGills was the first of what officials hoped would be many. It was predicted that one-hundred additional loans would be forthcoming for farms in the next four years, and all the loans would go to "building good communities, churches and schools", all by way of insuring "the future."

Within months of the end of hostilities, millions of servicemen were on their way home. It was a frightening time for many, uncertain how they would fit into the world that was unfolding. Others were just glad to leave the service behind, to get back to sweethearts and wives and families. To become a civilian again was a wondrous thing. It was a time of new beginnings.

Much of what would occur in the coming months was built on foundations set in place before the war. Take McGill. Born in South Dakota in 1923, he settled in Smock in 1940, after driving his mother, Kate, a native of the Dawson-Broadford portion of the county, half way across the country in order to attend a relative's funeral. John's decision to stay once he was here seems a bit curious, inasmuch as he had a stake in South Dakota as the owner of some livestock he had left behind. But it was his nature to put down roots. Besides, he had a cash problem. When he and his mom left South Dakota in the family's Chevy truck, they had the sum total of $150, most of that earned by John at a livestock auction in Sioux City, Iowa. The drive east was costly, and by the time mother and son got to Pennsylvania, they had a paltry $10.

John went to work, hauling special-delivery groceries for the company store in Smock. On one such delivery, to company house number 276, he met Kathryn, whose father, Charles Crosson, was a coal miner and would secure John a mining job at the Maxwell Mine in Washington County.

With the war at high tide, John was drafted. Because of extra pay, he volunteered for the 17th Airborne Division forming at Camp McCall, South Carolina. Thrown in as green troops during the last great German offensive of the war in December 1944, the division helped break the enemy encirclement of Bastogne. Captured by Germans inside a barn, McGill and three other Americans jumped their captors, managing to overpower and, in John's words, "eliminate" them. On the 10th of January 1945, John McGill fell asleep in a freshly dug foxhole. Three feet of snow covered the ground, and it was bitterly cold. He awoke in a hospital bed in England with wounds to his head, shoulders, and legs, and no recollection of what hit him. Waking to fresh sheets and light streaming through a nearby window, John's first thought was that he was dead and in heaven.

John spent four months in the hospital. Afterward, he was attached to the Office of Military Government in Berlin. Far from being the bombed rubble heap others saw, John considered Berlin paradise - a "gambler's paradise." In six weeks' time, McGill staked himself to a hefty bankroll thanks to his participation in the flourishing blackmarket, where even a cartoon of cigarettes fetched a pretty price. McGill claimed he sold an unsuspecting Russian soldier a Mickey Mouse watch for an astounding $1,500, and then sold him another one, as a substitute for the first. The average Russian soldier, McGill found, "was a very uneducated person, so uneducated they didn't even know how to wind a watch." Encouraged by the Army to re-enlist, McGill joked to a superior that six more months in Berlin would make him a millionaire or send him to jail. He chose to get out.

His intention from the very start was to buy a farm. Shortly after returning home, he ran into a nephew of Rosencram Powell, who told McGill the old man was looking to sell his place in Franklin Township. McGill knew Powell from before the war. His mother and father had rented from Powell. It wasn't long before John was able to strike a deal.

McGill worked hard on the farm. He had to. The McGill family was growing, eventually to six boys and three girls. With the kids and all and with new farm equipment to pay for, John found himself in a financial bind. To fix things, one day in 1951 he ventured over to McKeesport to see if he might find a second job at the U.S. Steel National Tube plant. Never afraid of long hours, McGill practically demanded work. "Tell me right now if I can get a job here," he roared. For the next 32 years minus the occasional strike or lay off, he labored literally around the clock, putting in sixteen, seventeen, eighteen hours days between the mill and farm. So intent was he to hold on to his plot of earth that he turned down a chance to become a foreman or even assistant plant superintendent at the U.S. Steel Fairless Hills plant near Philadelphia.

Their horrid memories of the war notwithstanding, many veterans felt they had no choice but to plod forward, taking one small step at a time. Walter Radishek felt this way. A native of Perryopolis, Radishek joined the first class of what what was called the Uniontown Center, a branch of Waynesburg College especially created to enroll ex-GIs eager for a college degree paid for by the government. More than 250 men and women, the vast majority of them veterans, signed up for the fall semester 1946.

The "campus" was confined to the basement and part of the first floor of the Ella Peach Elementary School, an elegant three-story building one block south of Main at the corner of Church Street and Gallatin Avenue. With the college trustees deciding only in July to proceed with the opening, arrangements were made in haste, and it showed. Hugh Barclay, chosen to teach history and himself a veteran, recalled the school was still being assembled just weeks before classes met. The small faculty and staff (a total of 11) begged and borrowed chairs, tables, desks; in other words, the essentials.

Veterans like Radishek, Henry DiVirgilio of Perryopolis, and Dan Reilly of Uniontown hardly noticed. Radishek was happy to attend any school, though he had letters of acceptance from Notre Dame and Penn State. Why did he choose the Uniontown Center? Two factors, really: money and convenience. Radishek along with DiVirgilio were among nearly a dozen former servicemen from Perryopolis who threw in their lot with the Uniontown Center and Waynesburg College. Every morning the men piled into cars for the trek south on Route 51.

Radishek's experience is instructive, for out of the tragedy of war his life was transformed. After graduating from Perry High School in 1936 in the midst of the Depression, he spent the next several years barely eking out a living. After trying and failing to find work in the steel mills, he settled for work in the mines, first at Gates and later at Edenborn, both long drives from Perryopolis, where he continued to live with his mother, father, and brother. Later, he became a timberman at Banning Mine followed by a job hauling stone for a truck outfit that had snagged a contract with the local office of the Works Progress Administration, a creation of the Roosevelt administration. Radishek's last job before being drafted was at Whitsett coal mine.

A gangling youth with a shock of red hair, Radishek entered the service in 1942. Two years later, he was in Italy, helping to relieve the Anzio beachhead; eventually, his unit, the 85th Division, participated in the capture of Rome. Afterward, he crossed the mountains near Florence. In October 1944, during a firefight with a German patrol in which nine of his buddies died, Staff Sergeant Radishek was wounded; shrapnel collapsed one lung and ripped open a leg. His last thought before losing consciousness was of home.

Radishek spent several months in an Army hospital in Memphis, Tennessee, before receiving his discharge. It was a cold February morning in 1945 when the bus from Pittsburgh pulled to a stop on Route 51. Radishek hobbled off. Home was a quarter mile away. The ex-soldier with damaged lungs and a bum leg spent the next hour getting there. He spent all of 1945 and most of the following year recuperating.

Sometime in the spring or summer of 1946, Radishek and several friends called on the Veterans Administration representative who held office hours in Perryopolis once a week. The VA man sat back in his chair and asked, "Well, what do you fellas want to do?"

Radishek had an idea about going to college. He and a buddy, Andy Huzinec, had been up to see Penn State. Alone he had visited West Virginia University in Morgantown and Dickinson College in Carlisle. As for a major, he had given business administration some thought, especially if he could tie that into agriculture. His father and his brother Ralph were part-time farmers.

How practical an idea was college? Could he make the grade? At 28, Radishek's high school years were a distant memory. He had liked school, but had only been a fair student. College, he knew, would be harder yet.

But if not college, then what? Given his physical limitations, coal mining was out of the question as was steel mill work. "I made up my mind I was going to study," he recalled. "It was either do or die."

Henry DiVirgilio was in much the same boat as his good friend Radishek. Twenty-six-years-old in 1946, DiVirgilio was a Navy veteran, having served on a repair ship in the Pacific. He had felt lucky getting into the Navy, which he much preferred to the Army.

After dropping out of high school in 1935, DiVirgilio had enrolled in the Civilian Conservation Corps, a New Deal agency that gave unemployed young men temporary work. Assigned to a CCC camp in Arizona for a year (and sending most of his pay home for support of his family), DiVirgilio returned to Perryopolis in 1936, getting work in one of the steel mills near Pittsburgh. Later, he drove truck for a living. Eventually, though, he did something extraordinary: DiVirgilio returned to high school. Studying like mad, he completed two years' work in one. He also met a pretty senior, his future wife, Betsy.

Henry's first instinct following the war was to go back to his old steel mill job at Clairton. The more he thought about it, however, the more his mind turned to college. He was listening to Betsy, who knew how hard her own father worked as a miner. Besides, Henry was bright enough for college, or so it seemed to Betsy. A lot of this backed up what Henry was thinking and feeling. He recalled his father's years in the mines. For years, the DiVirgilio family was in hock to the company store. Tending the fields on his in-law's farm, Henry felt like an Amish laborer. It was all muscle and strain and sweat. Henry thought to himself, "I've got to try college."

His first choice, the University of Pittsburgh, turned him down. Henry had his sights set on an engineering degree, but Pitt officials determined he lacked the background in math to get into their program. He was devastated, but with Betsy urging him on, he eventually applied to the new Uniontown Center of Waynesburg College, where he became a member of the inaugural class, majoring in education.

Radishek, DiVirgilio, and millions of other veterans

were the beneficiaries of a far-sighted government program called the GI Bill of Rights. Congress passed the GI Bill in June 1944, a few weeks after the successful landing in Normandy by Allied forces. As President Roosevelt was signing the legislation at an informal ceremony at the White House (declaring the bill "gives emphatic notice to the men and women of our armed forces that the American people do not intend to let them down"), U.S. troops were moving against the German-held coastal city of Cherbourg, France. Around the same time, many of the experts charged with divining the future were worried, for the nation's post-war prospects appeared fairly grim.

"It is self-evident that the re-integration of war veterans cannot take place successfully unless the veterans get jobs," wrote a serviceman himself, Army Lieutenant Charles G. Bolte, in *The Nation.* "If they don't get jobs, there's going to be trouble ... bad trouble. The fact is, most service men - and women - do not look forward to becoming civilians, that is to say, citizens." A government survey found that 65 percent of service personnel expected a post-war depression. A Senate committee concluded that the end of the war meant the loss of some eight million jobs while "thousands of manufacturers (would be) rendered insolvent. ... The general level of production ... will fall sharply."

Politicians in general were haunted by the specter of the early 1930s, the years of the bonus armies. These bedraggled ex-servicemen, left shipwrecked by the Great Depression, marched on state legislatures, demanding compensation for their sacrifices from hard-pressed public treasuries. They marched on Washington, too, where they were dispersed by force of arms.

Was this the fate that awaited the veterans of Normandy, of Iwo Jima, of North Africa?

As early as 1942, the Roosevelt administration began to take a look at the potential problems of peace. By 1944, much of the apparatus of the federal government seemed geared to finding ways to ease the path of returning veterans. Between July 1, 1944, and June 30, 1945, no less than 2,800 veterans bills were introduced in Congress. It was a political free-for-all. The competition between the two parties for the allegiance of the veterans became fierce, the *New York Times* running a cartoon of a befuddled GI being yanked in one direction by the Republican elephant and in the opposite direction by the Democratic donkey.

It was easy to be cynical about all of this, and many were, including *The Nation*. One of the magazine's writers was on Capitol Hill as the Allies were streaming ashore in Normandy and came away with the impression that congressmen were politicians first and policy makers second. "What day is this?" he had the average member of Congress asking himself. "D-Day? What has that got to do with us? Our men are landing on the beaches of Normandy. But will they vote in November?"

Despite the cynicism, Congress managed to act. By the fall of 1946, first President Roosevelt and then President Truman along with lawmakers had constructed a first line of defense for veterans.

Of course, the expectation was that veterans would help themselves. The message GIs heard time and again was: get on with your life. Full-page newspaper ads fairly screamed the message. One such ad in a Uniontown newspaper asked in bold lettering: "DO YOU WANT - a college, trade or business school education?" The ad was actually directed at getting men into the service, but it served just as well to remind ex-soldiers of the rewards of the GI Bill and of life as a civilian.

The post-war world, it was becoming clear, was not going to be a bed of roses. The press carried the story of a former GI and his family living in Central Park after having been tossed from their New York City apartment for want of rent money. And there was the occasional mug shot in the newspaper of some battle-hardened veteran re-enlisting after failing to find a job.

There were even reminders, unintended though they may have been, that the veteran was lucky to be alive. In July 1946, Lieutenant Grant Warren Smith of Farmington was declared dead after being listed as missing in action for a year. Private Luther E. Garletts, whose mother Ella lived in Dunbar, was memorialized in the newspaper with his photograph and a few lines of type reminding readers he had fallen in action in Italy two years earlier.

Fortunate was the veteran who returned

home. One such veteran was "Pinky" Brown. Head football coach at North Union High School, Brown resigned his position with an eye on attending college under the GI Bill and becoming a dentist.

Onward and upward.

In time Henry DiVirgilio transferred from the Uniontown Center to Waynesburg College proper. By then he and Betsy were husband and wife. Sharing rent and space with another Perryopolis couple on an apartment in Waynesburg, Henry and Betsy soon welcomed their baby girl, Diane.

Diane became ill with a milk allergy that went undiagnosed for months. Mounting doctor bills prompted Henry to quit school and to go to work at the Clairton steel mill. But having come so far and done so well in his quest to further his education, Henry and Betsy jointly decided he should try to finish his degree, which he did, in 1951, the same year he was hired to teach at Frazier High School in Perryopolis.

Betsy would later say, "I don't think (Henry) ever felt a college education was due him. We appreciated what the government did."

But the DiVirgilios had worked hard, too.

A sense of time slipping away was common to many veterans. Certainly Dan Reilly felt that way. Lanky with a long, lean face, Reilly went to war and returned home all before his 21st birthday. Unlike Radishek and DiVirgilio, Dan always expected to be a college man, a fact made clear to him by his father, a Uniontown attorney.

Indeed, even before graduating from high school, Reilly was off to college, plucked from Uniontown and sent by the Army to Lexington, Virginia, for classes in engineering. In a matter of months, however, Reilly and most of his classmates were shipped off campus for infantry training. The fighting in Europe was proving to be enormously costly in terms of lives lost. In practically no time Reilly was headed to the battlefront.

Looking back years later, Dan noted that "it took thirteen days from the time I left home from basic training to the front line. ... We never stopped. We went from boat to train to trucks to walking." It seemed to the youngster that he had just gotten out of high school and here he was in combat facing the enemy.

A member of the 94th Division, Dan saw action in France, Germany, and Czechoslovakia. Wearing the same muddy, wet socks day after day, Reilly contracted a severe case of trench foot. Sent to the rear for treatment, his war was over.

The GI Bill was a godsend for Reilly. With four bothers all expected to attend college, the government's largesse was a welcome addition to the Reilly family finances.

A good, if not, outstanding student in high school, Reilly was amused more than annoyed at being required to take a test to determine his occupational aptitude, as a qualification for the GI Bill. The public servant who administered the test insistently asked the young veteran if he was dead-set on becoming a lawyer. Each time, Reilly answered that a law degree was what he wanted and what he meant to earn.

Reilly's decision to attend the Waynesburg Center in Uniontown was based on simple economics: the school was within waking distance of the family home on Gallatin Avenue. In addition to easing his transportation worries (the family owned but one car), he would eat and sleep at home, saving money as well.

Classes were small and intimate at the Center, the college men and women seeing very little of the grade school students who occupied the greater part of Ella Peach School. Robert J. Bowden. a quietly efficient assistant professor of English, was named associate dean and Center director while Vivian Hughes, one of the few experienced instructors, was appointed assistant dean of women. Anthony Christobek, Hugh Barclay's college roommate, taught chemistry and Morgan Orgent and Floyd Forsthe were math instructors. Elizabeth Eisaman, recently out of college and attractive enough to catch the eye of many of the former GIs, joined Bowden in the English department. Charles Farrell, a former public school teacher who during the war had studied the flight of birds in an effort to perfect glider plane technology, taught biology. The history instructor was Barclay, whose bow ties and tall frame quickly become campus landmarks.

Skepticism about the new venture was rife,

not least at Waynesburg College proper. These standard-bearers of academia had a hard time accepting former soldiers into their midst. What kind of students would they be? "Waynesburg standards were rather rigid," Barclay recalled. "They weren't willing to take anybody much on condition." The GI Bill loosened things up a bit.

Barclay, a native of Carmichaels in Greene County, was himself an example of the hardy, can-do spirit of the veterans who gathered at the Center. A weather observer with the 8th Air Force in India and Burma, he was at church one Sunday morning in 1947 when the pastor, the Reverend Harry Gardner, a Waynesburg College vice president, whispered in his ear about a job opening in Uniontown. Would he be interested? Barclay was staggered at Gardner's proposal that he teach history - European history, no less. It never entered his mind that he was cut out for such a thing. A science major at Waynesburg College before the war, Barclay had been dabbling in his father's real estate business, searching like a lot of veterans to find his way.

It always puzzled him why Gardner approached him. "I was not a brilliant student," he recalled. "I was far from being one of the glamor boys on campus. ... I didn't play football."

Tackling his new assignment with trepidation, Barclay bought an unabridged dictionary and then combed through the textbook three or four times, outlining important passages and trying to commit as much as possible to memory. It was quite a sweep of history he was taking on: from about 300 A.D. to 1500. The second semester started with the Reformation. "It was sink or swim," he remembered.

No one had much of an idea of what to expect. Some experts predicted disaster, that college standards would decline, that the veteran himself would not learn a thing, either because the instruction would be inferior or the students themselves would not be up to the task.

In fact, there was heavy going at the Uniontown seat of higher learning. Barclay wasn't the only teacher picked virtually off the street and sent to the head of the class. As for the students, Barclay recalled some of them really struggling to make the grade. Many were just back from the battlefield, some with meager academic backgrounds. Buckling down was doubly hard for those who hadn't cracked a book in years. More than a few students complained to Barclay about having to plow through the history text. And if they were asked to speak in class, many froze. It was worse than facing the enemy, they said. Barclay, hardly a poised figure himself, tried to be encouraging. Still, he didn't let up. He insisted, bottom line, that students pay attention, do the reading, and pass the tests.

The former soldiers, sailors, and Marines were eager beyond anyone's expectations. There were so many more students than anyone anticipated that at first there weren't enough textbooks. The science lab equipment didn't arrive until late fall. Complaints were few, however, and classes were always full. No student appeared shell-shocked, listless, or indifferent. Instead, the air was electric with high-hopes.

It was a veterans' world in the fall of 1946. Just as the former GIs were settling down to study in October, lovely Donna Reed arrived, cinematically, at the Penn Theater (at the corner of Main Street and Beeson Boulevard in Uniontown) starring in *Faithful In My Fashion,* co-starring Tom Drake who had "dreamed" of meeting someone like Donna "for four long years." Darker was *Till The End of Time* with Guy Madison, Robert Mitchum, and Dorothy McGuire, the story of a hard readjustment to civilian life. Of course, some entertainment was pure escapism, such as *If I'm Lucky*, a "joyous hit" with "Hit Parade Songs" and a young crooner, former Canonsburg barber Perry Como, in a leading role. At the Club York between Uniontown and Smithfield, a singer described as "Charles Chaplin's protégé", Joan Barry, was appearing live along with master of ceremonies Dick Martin, the future star of TV's *Laugh-In*.

Appearing live at Red Cross headquarters in Uniontown were thirty war brides. Local radio personality Charlie Underwood spoke. Across town, at 71 Murray Avenue, veteran Peter Panos, who had served with a field artillery unit in Europe, introduced the local press to a Greek woman, a guest in his house, Despina Mauropolou. She spoke gravely of Nazi atrocities which she had seen and experienced as a concentration camp prisoner. She was bitter beyond words. She said female prisoner such as a herself "could not protect ourselves against their .. lust" nor their murderous ways.

Americans were worried about a next war, about patriotism (relative to communism), and about politics in 1946. Late in the summer, a large crowd gathered at Coker Stadium in Connellsville for an "Americanism" rally. It heard General William E. Hall talk about keeping "the American way of life." One sure way, he said, was to have an army, navy and air force strong enough to deter aggression. General Hall was not assuming "there would be another war." On the contrary, "I'm thoroughly convinced that if we are adequately prepared, there won't be another war."

It appeared domestic communism was an ugly fact of life. Or was the "Red peril" a figment of overwrought imaginations fed by the glimmer of political advantage? George Bloom, executive secretary to Pennsylvania Governor Edward Martin, declared, "I have seen individuals in Harrisburg inciting good American soldiers ... (who were) being lead into demands on our state government that reek with communism. ... These fine young men and women are not thinking straight, because they were too willing to be lead blindly without thinking and therefore do not realize what they are doing and what it means to them in the end."

A Minnesota Republican, Senator Joseph Ball, before speaking to a GOP rally at the Fayette County courthouse, let it be known that "old-line Democrats, dissatisfied with the communistic trends within their own party and anxious to join in an effort to improve national conditions" were "invited" to attend.

County Democrats answered: "The local GOP would have you believe that if you vote Democratic, you're voting communistic." The Republican party was being "crudely expedient ... with its idiotic, asinine slogans begging the intelligence and even patriotism of voters."

President Truman's poll numbers reflected the impact of the Republican charges and the state of national well-being brought on by the end of the war. In May 1945, a month after succeeding Franklin Roosevelt (and amidst the euphoria of victory in Europe), Harry Truman's popularity stood at 85 percent. A little over a year later that number had been halved.

It seemed nearly everyone had a complaint against the Office of Price Administration (OPA), or, as a Hopwood grocer recommended, the Office of People's Aversion. Of particular interest were controls on the cost of meat, which accounted, some said, for the current meat shortage. Miners complained loudly, UMWA District 4 president Mike Harris rasping, "I don't understand how the miners are going to work without meat. It is impossible - they must have meat. ... Jelly and egg sandwiches" just would not do. Fayette County miners were soon echoing their union brethren in Somerset County: "No meat, no work." They appealed to John L. Lewis.

In August 1946, the OPA approved price increases for oranges, warm-air furnaces, toilet paper, woolen booties, eyeglass lenses, copper coil, compressors, cast iron radiators, cotton hosiery, table linen, rope, twine, and passenger car tires. In October, after meat producers were rightfully blamed for holding livestock off the market, President Truman ordered the end of controls on meat. If this was a last minute stab at regaining ground before the congressional elections, it didn't work. Truman's popularity continued to plunge.

An order raising the price of building materials was too late to help the county add the General Cigar Company to its employer ranks. The Uniontown Chamber of Commerce bargained for months to secure the plant and the employment of 400 workers. The deal fell through when, according to everyone concerned, it was discovered that building materials were not available, and wouldn't be for another year, if then.

How many of the cigar plant jobs might have gone to disabled veterans no one could say. What was know was this: there were at least 75 ex-GIs, many of them crippled for life, who were anxious to find work or training for work but could find neither. A plea to employers went out from M. W. McDonald of the Veterans Administration: "Our (training) program is worthless if the disabled veteran cannot find employment. We appeal to you to lend a hand."

All of this, plus scores of other factors,

including rumblings from John L. Lewis about government oversight of the mines, had a bearing on the campaign for Congress, pitting Democrat John Rankin, a Fayette County commissioner, against Republican William E. Crow, the handsome, silver-haired ex-mayor of Uniontown and the son of the late U.S. Senator William Crow.

Rankin and Crow were possibilities at all because of the death a year earlier of Democratic congressman J. Buell Snyder. The "father of the super highway" left some big shoes to fill, and it was not clear either Rankin or Crow could fill them. As things turned out, it was a quiet campaign, in the sense that hardly anything uttered by the candidates found its way into print. Snyder, one suspects, would have been all over Fayette and Somerset counties. Not Crow and Rankin, who were content to let the party bosses talk for them. Not even the appearance in the county of Republican Governor Edward Martin, on his way to the Senate in Washington by way of a smashing victory over incumbent Senator Guffey, could pry a comment from Crow. In the end, Crow defeated Rankin by less than 4,00 votes, thanks to his showing in Fayette County. Snyder had carried Fayette County by 11,000 votes in 1944. Rankin managed only a 2,000 vote margin in 1946.

More than a few veterans just back from the war were still thinking of their former comrades. In this regard, discussion ensued about separate tributes for two Fayette County natives who had especially superior war records: Medal of Honor winner Alfred Wilson of Fairchance, a medical corpsman killed in Europe, and General of the Army George C. Marshall.

It was suggested that land in the Fairchance area be set aside as a "living memorial" to Wilson; perhaps some suitable land close to his home could be designated as a state park.

Marshall was serving in China at the time, attempting to patch together a political deal between the Chinese government and the communists. The local Amvets, organized in April, had asked and received permission to name their post for Marshall. In June 1946, writing from Nanking, Marshall addressed Amvets commander Robert E. Rutter. He thanked the veterans for extending to him an Amvets membership, noting rather formally, "I accept this generous evidence of your goodwill."

It's not clear if Raymond Rutter, commander at American Legion Post 51 on Gallatin Avenue in Uniontown, broached the subject of a Marshall commemoration to the honoree himself, a Post 51 "life member." Rutter had no immediate idea what form a Marshall tribute might take, and so he proposed that civc, fraternal, and "patriotic" leaders meet in order to devise a plan of action. He called Marshall a "great man."

Not all tributes were local. A young Belgium woman wrote to the parents of Paul A. Danko of the countryside around Smithfield. Killed in March 1945 at the age of 18 while serving with the 4th Infantry Division, Danko lay in a grave not far from the girl's home. She had recently taken upon herself the solemn duty of caring for the grave. She told the family in a letter, "The cemetery is very peaceful and good looking. I often go there to take flowers."

Not all veterans were heroes. In September, police arrested three ex-servicemen accused of robbing and beating an elderly Ohiopyle couple at the couple's home. Twenty-three year old Charles Gates and James Welch, 22, both of Connellsville, and twenty-four year old Varen Joseph of Ohiopyle, said they did it because they were drunk. One of the men explained his behavior by saying, "I thought the whole thing was a joke."

Late in the 20th century, the social critic Michael Barone would observe that Americans in the post-war years "acted with a confidence in the future which the Americans of 1940 had pretty much lost. They married and had children (when) less than a decade before they would not have dared to make such commitments. They bought houses, although the depression had taught them the value of housing could collapse and equity could could be totally wiped out. In August 1945, they had learned suddenly that the war was over. (Soon) they began to understand that prosperity and economic growth were not over and would continue."

Well, maybe. The fact is in 1946 there was a lot of hemming and hawing, especially about this matter of buying a home. As far back as 1944, months before the end of the war, there had risen a steady drumbeat about the coming housing shortage and what was to be done about it, and whether veterans should rent or buy, and what role the government should or should not play. There was some discussion that the housing provisions of the GI Bill were flawed. One critic claimed the legislation was "mystifying" and predicted ruin for untold millions of veterans if they were goaded into buying homes they could not afford due to high interest rates and maintenance costs. Charles Abram, a professor at the New School for Social Research in New York City, called for a "grace period for defaulting veterans" as well as "adequate planning" by communities to ward off "early obsolescence and blight."

Mindful of the shortcomings, Congress increased the GI Bill's housing loan guarantee from $2,000 to $4,000. According to VA director Omar Bradley, the "VA guarantee fully protected" the lender and enabled builders to offer a veteran a house for "nothing down.'"

The national American Legion's Paul Griffith was not satisfied. Griffith insisted veterans should rent rather than buy. Like Professor Abram, he feared many veterans would be pushed onto a financial limb from which there was only one exit. Housing was the veteran's "hottest problem," Griffith said, and the lack of housing was "approaching a national scandal." Attending a Jewish War Veterans conference, Griffith heard Louis Bennett, a regional official of the National Housing Agency, tell the gathering that even though there would be one million new housing starts by the end of 1946, veterans should insist on the continuation of construction and rent controls, "if they want housing for themselves" instead of "mansions" for the few. Bennett concluded that veterans should oppose "Alice-in-Wonderland arguments", such as calls to lift controls, which were periodically issued "in the guise of helping veterans."

It was hard to figure what to do. One example of the confusion occurred when it was reported that groundbreaking was taking place on 42 "veterans' homes" near the Benjamin Franklin Junior High School in the vicinity of Lawn Avenue and Union

Street and along Sycamore and Show Streets in South Union. Called the Veterans' Community Center, the development appeared to have the official blessings of the American Legion. The name of the chairman of the Post 51 housing committee, R. C. McGee Jr., was mentioned in several of the news stories about the project. It was reliably reported that the Uniontown Planning Commission had approved the project, and 400 "survey forms" had been received by the Post. It sounded wonderful: the homes were to contain four to six rooms, with heating, plumbing, and "kitchen arrangements" already figured in.

But most of this wasn't true. Legion officials quickly distanced themselves from the project, one of them declaring the Legion "can not ... participate in or endorse any project in private gain to a private individual or a group of individuals. ... The Legion is only interested in civic betterment, good government, and real Americanism." Not only that but the city planning commission had never endorsed the project. In fact, that body seems to have rejected it, hands down. There were several problems, including "gullies", "poor planning (too many dead end streets), "no provision" made for "sewage disposal", and restricted "ingress and egress." Overall, the project didn't "lend itself for development of Craig farm as part of the city."

A day after this report appeared McGee confessed there had been some confusion about the role of the American Legion, but asserted that as an ex-servicemen and as a member of the Post committee assigned to examine the housing situation, it was never his intent to use the "Legion name" to promote the project. He said his interest had been sparked by the "many pathetic letters" received in response to the Legion survey of veterans' housing needs. He personally thought that a veterans' housing plan was a good idea, since it would promote unity and neighborliness among individuals "of the same age ... who have something in common as a result of their war service ... and with children of the same age. The Craig farm offered the best possibility. ... We are willing to do everything possible to get housing before winter. ... Through the GI loan provisions, we had hoped to be able, by our own initiative, to obtain homes for ourselves."

That housing was needed was clear enough. "Temporary housing" for 49 families was going up near Connellsville, the buildings coming from the Army's Camp Shenango in Greenville, Mercer County. But here, too, there were problems. The carpenters working on the project went on strike, wanting 65-cents an hour in pay. The non-union carpenters made their appeal through county detective Lawrence Hagerty, who in turn contacted Thomas McIntyre, the district chief of unionized construction workers.

Easy-to-assemble homes were being sold in North Union Township, along North Gallatin Avenue Extension. One- and two-bedroom models were available for "immediate delivery" for a small down payment and modest monthly payments. Or so said the advertisement, which boasted that the homes featured "modernized early American styling ... comfortable proportions and convenient floor plans." Workers were available to put up these homes on land already purchased or homeowners could "save hundreds of dollars" by doing some of their own work.

Here, certainly, was an example of the U.S.

economy at work, adapting itself to changing conditions. During the Great Depression, home construction took a nose dive. But even before that, during the prosperous 1920s for example, individual homeownership was never a big thing, or as big a thing as it would later become. The typical mortgage was then expected to be paid off in five to ten years, with 30 percent down and interest rates in the range of six to eight percent. During the thirties, the Roosevelt administration tried to reverse some of these figures, but it took the postwar years and the GI Bill to settle the matter in favor of the middle class investor, Mr. and Mrs. Average American.

The postwar years also solved the problem of who was to build the housing veterans were clamoring for. The Depression had driven most home builders out of business. Except for the wealthy, home construction came to a screeching halt, a condition that persisted through the war years, when all things military took precedent. It worried some critics that home-building expertise and experience were missing. Such fears were groundless, especially when there were men like Charles Hileman around.

A native of Bruceton Mills, West Virginia, Hileman moved with his family to Uniontown in the 1930s, first settling in the Union Street area and later moving to Whitman Avenue on the east end of town. A lanky youth, Hileman graduated from Uniontown High School in 1943. In August of that year, he entered the service. By the following October Hileman was in France, assigned to the 4th Armored Division, 8th Tank Battalion. He was a tank "loader", responsible for loading ammunition, principally 76 mm. and 35 mm. shells to fire at Germans.

He was injured twice, the first time after just 11 days in combat. The second incident occurred Easter Sunday 1945 while assaulting German troops holed up in a village. Hileman's tank and three others become lost. Almost by accident, they encountered a superior German force and got into a brief exchange of fire. Hileman, wielding a 50-caliber machine gun, was aiming at tiny German heads that flashed occasionally from entrenched positions when, what he took to be a bazooka shell, struck a nearby tree, spraying chunks of wood and shrapnel in all directions. Hileman looked down and saw a hole the size of a half-dollar in his arm. He spent the next several months in the hospital. By the time he got out the war in Europe was long over, and the young man, who admitted to being scared to death the entire time he was in combat, was on his way home. He ended the fateful year 1945 at the altar, marrying his hometown sweetheart, Thelma Barnhart, who had graduated from South Union High School. Hileman was almost - but not quite - 21-years-old.

Private Hileman had managed to save $1,500 during the war, so the newlyweds had something at least. Charles took a job at his uncle's gas station in Fredericktown, Washington County, for which he was paid $100 a month. Meanwhile, his father Clyde Hileman, a carpenter who had gotten the family through the Depression by working odd jobs, got involved with putting up the so-called Gunnison homes that were being built in the Gallatin Avenue Extension area, in what until then had been a grassy, rolling field. The pre-fabricated houses came in four sections 24- to 40-feet in length, with side panels four feet wide and eight feet high, and all of it bolted together on a concrete floor. It soon became apparent that demand for these homes was such that Clyde Hileman would need help keeping up. He put out a call to his two sons, Charles and Gail.

"People said those houses wouldn't be there more than a year or two," Charles recalled decades later. "They said the wind would blow them down. 'Oh, those little crackerjack houses won't survive,' that's what they said."

For the next 16 years constructing Gunnisons was just about all that Charles Hileman did. Working as private contractors for a division of U.S. Steel, the Hilemans built these homes which some people said looked like shoe boxes with front stoops in North Union Township as well as in Pittsburgh, Greensburg, Perryopolis, and Harrisburg. "We were going full blast, there was so much work," Hileman remembered. On one occasion, the Hilemans put up a Gunnison home in the new Craig Meadows development, on land the American Legion had disputed.

In an odd twist, the man who built homes

never stayed in one home for very long himself. The Hilemans after returning from Fredericktown moved into a place on McClellandtown Road in South Union, a small three-room affair that cost $3,000. They then moved to Dixon Boulevard, followed by rental property on Cleveland Avenue. After returning from Harrisburg in 1956 or so, Charles and Thelma took up residence on Eggleston, then Connor, then Hookton Avenue, and finally on Kerr Street, the last a duplex.

Charles Hileman considered himself a good Christian, a born-again Christian, and attended, with Thelma, the First Brethren Church on Union Street. The church pastor was Henry G. Rempel, a slightly-built man with protruding ears and keen sense of how to promote church growth. It occurred to Rempel that a new Sunday School class, one that appealed to young married couples, just might encourage returning veterans and their spouses to attend church services together and become dedicated church members. Thus was born, in the fall of 1945, the Philathea Class. In addition to the Hilemans, some of the other early members were Jack and Mabel Hostetler; Jack owned and operated Hostetler Jewelers, at the corner of Main and Morgantown streets in Uniontown. Bill and Helen Robbins; Bill worked with his brother Bob at Robbins Market in Connellsville. Stenson and Ruth Gail Edenfield; Stenson was a Hagan's Ice Cream man, an expert in refrigeration. Lee and Dorothy Collier; Lee worked at Metzler's Department Store, downtown, in the appliance department; and Ed and Jeanne Churby. Ed labored at Hankin and Paulson Lumberyard on North Beeson Boulevard in Uniontown.

The men and women of the Philathea Class were an eclectic, sometimes restless bunch. Most had growing families, children born during or just after the war, and all had to figure out how to make their way in the new world that dawned with the end of the fighting. It was never easy, though most managed to leaven their lives with good humor and optimism, perhaps as a result of their faith in an ultimate, heavenly reward. Not even the cruelest of blows, the death of their son Jim from muscular dystrophy, dimmed permanently the enthusiasm for life of the Churbys, who resided with daughter Wendy Jean on Woodlawn Avenue, not far from the South Union High School football stadium. The two-story, six-room house, costing $9,500, was purchased on the strength of a GI loan in 1959.

Ed Churby, who served on the amphibious personnel carrier the USS *Elizabeth B. Stanton* in the Pacific during the war, was not alone in taking his time in purchasing a place. It sometimes took a fellow a while to find the nerve, even if he had the money.

One ex-serviceman with cash in his pocket was Lee Collier. Lee had managed to pad his account thanks primarily to his enterprising ways in the Navy, which he entered in May 1944 after spending the first part of the war at a plant in Connecticut building the small carried-based plane the F4U Corsair. Owing to a draft exemption (the Colliers were parents to two daughters, both born after Pearl Harbor), Lee stayed stateside, working at both the Connecticut airplane factory and at the steel mill in Homstead, until his draft status changed. The mill job was a miserable undertaking, as far as Lee was concerned: the work was dirty and hot, and he was always being moved from shift to shift, daylight to night-turn. It was hard to settle into a routine. In addition, there was the everyday automobile trip from Uniontown to Homestead, a journey Lee found repetitive and time-consuming, even if he did share a ride with an uncle and a brother-in-law. In Connecticut, Lee worked on the hydraulic parts of the Corsair: the folding wings, the retractable landing gear, the gun charges.

"When I went in the service, things were very serious," Lee remembered. "They needed replacement (soldiers), and regardless of my situation (at home), I was drafted."

Presented with a choice, the Army or Navy, Lee picked the Navy. He looked forward to getting a job on the Corsair (flown by Marines but maintained by the Navy), since he obviously knew the plane pretty well. Instead, he was shipped off to duty on an LST, short for Landing Ship Tank, a monstrous contraption capable of carrying 18 tanks or 500 tons of cargo and of pulling right up to a beach and unloading. LST duty was mostly boring, always uncomfortable, and largely without reward, and certainly without glory. Lee's craft, LST 609, unloaded equipment on Guam and Saipan, and got caught in some terrible sea storms, including a typhoon or two. Otherwise, there was time for the crew to explore the exotic islands of New Hebrides, a military staging area east of Australia and proximate to the Solomon Islands and Guadalcanal.

Pretty quickly, Lee discovered it was possible to trade with the island natives, whose diet included heaping portions of sea turtle. Lee used the turtles' shells to fashion bracelets and necklaces which he sent to Dorothy back home in Uniontown. His buddies took notice, and they asked Lee to fix them up an order for their wives and girlfriends. Lee soon had a thriving little business. By the time he was ready to leave the Pacific, he had mailed Dorothy over $1,000 in profits. Dorothy didn't spend a dime of this money, socking it away instead for the future. Lee arrived home on January 1, 1946, a slightly wealthier man than when he had started out.

It was to be expected that the Colliers would

Postwar: Children of the First Brethren Church

put a down payment on a new home in a jiffy. But it didn't happen. They evidently were listening to the likes of Paul Griffith, who cautioned veterans not to be rash, to rent instead of buy. It wasn't only Griffith. Lee heard the same from nearly everybody, and not just in 1946, but later, too. Be careful about the high price of things, people said. Now's not the time to build or buy. Meanwhile, the four Colliers moved in with Lee's mother at 254 Braddock Avenue, off Morgantown Street, in the vicinity of Ben Franklin Junior High School.

Three weeks after getting his discharge from the Navy, Lee headed off for work at Metzler's department store, situated across from the State Theater on Main Street in Uniontown.

Two factors led to Lee landing the Metzler's position. The first was his brother Jim, who worked there already and pulled some strings. The second was the GI Bill. Another provision of the bill provided for training wages. It worked this way: Lee's starting salary was $50 a week, half of which was paid by the government. Every six months, the government contributed $5 less to his pay and the department store $5 more. If everything worked out, after two-and-a-half years, Lee would be on the Metzler's payroll in the appliance department without a government subsidy. And that's exactly what happened.

Never, it appeared, had there been a more opportune time to be in the appliance business. The war had imposed severe restrictions on what could be manufactured and sold. Most everything had been funneled into the war effort.

Now a flood tide of consumer demand washed over the American economy, though few sensed in 1946 what was afoot. A Gallup poll late in 1945 suggested Americans were divided over whether business would be able to generate enough jobs for the millions of men receiving their military discharges. In 1945-46, the size of the military shrunk dramatically, from 12 million to 3 million, which effectively put 9 million unemployed men on the streets. The fuel that had fired the U.S. economy during the war, spending on the military, took a nosedive. The Pentagon budget practically collapsed, going from $81 billion in 1945 to $44 billion in 1946, and down to $13 billion in 1947, where it stayed for a while. And although the gross national product - the value of all goods and services in the U.S. - would hit the skids in 1947 at $258 billion, its lowest point since 1942, there were signs in 1946 that something strange and unexpected was about to happen. To take just one example, Detroit produced 2.1 million cars in 1946, representing an increase of 2500 percent! In short, America was about to enter the consumer age, and Lee Collier was at ground zero.

Lee recalled how anxious customers were to have their names placed on a waiting list for appliances, and how quickly incoming shipments - 30 to 40 appliances at a time - disappeared, as telephone calls were placed around town and around the county, alerting the lucky ones that their stove, their refrigerator, their washing machine had arrived. Would they be home for delivery?

Sometimes, the customer was disappointed, and this was when Lee appeared, tool box in hand, prepared to fix, or try to fix, what was wrong. Some appliances were just not reliable. The Frigidaire refrigerator a model of efficiency, an always humming piece of work? Guess again.

As Lee recalled, the government paid for his

shiny new set of tools, and Metzler's made sure he got the proper training, sending him every once in a while to a training session, frequently in Pittsburgh. Lee took a mail correspondence course for refrigeration.

And then there was that new appliance, television.

Bill Metzler, the store owner, was pretty skeptical about this TV business, not being sure how much of a splash television would make. After all, there was always radio. Eventually, he was persuaded to place a new Magnavox in the front display window facing Main Street. What happened next was a revelation. Daily, large crowds formed on the sidewalk outside the store. Soon, rows of straining necks and multitudinous eyes were fastened on the flickering, fuzzy images on the small screen. The crowds grew larger, until the police were compelled to ask management to please remove the set. Spilling onto the street, the mob had begun to hinder traffic. TV sales zoomed. Magnavox, Motorola, Dumont. Metzler's hardly had enough to keep up with demand.

There was one uncertainty about television, and it was a big deal. In a word, reception.

If you lived on a nice high hill, the clarity of the picture was good most of the time. Anywhere else, things were problematic. "Customers would come in and say my neighbor so-and-so up on Morgantown Street hill gets good reception. I don't," Lee recalled.

"Where do you live?" he remembered asking.

"Mount Vernon Avenue. Now if you can't fix this, you can take the set back. We don't want it. We can't see anything except snow."

"We had to counteract that," Lee said. "We hired a regular repairman for electronics. When I became service manager, we had eight fellows total for TV service and repair."

An antenna strategically placed on a rooftop was the answer to most reception problems. Installation was no walk in the park, however. During a brisk breeze or on an icy cold day, it was close to impossible. One day, in Revere, Lee and Bill Bell nearly froze to death while installing an antenna for the Rev. O'Brien. On another occasion, working atop a house near Dunbar, a sudden March wind came up. Snow clouds formed as the wind stiffened considerably. Finally, it became too much for Bell, who announced he couldn't hold the antenna much longer and was going to release it. "Bill, if you leave go, you're going with it," Lee answered gravely. Bill hung on, and they finished the job.

Despite the challenges, business was superb. In 1955, Bill Metzler bought out Peoples' Furniture store at the corner of Main Street and Gallatin Avenue, and moved the appliance department there.

In the meantime, the Collier family was growing. "Little Lee", as he was known, was born late in 1946, and Lynn came along in 1954. Still, there was no family home, though there was a lot which Lee and Dorothy had purchased with the $1,000 profit from the wartime sell of bracelets in the Pacific. It just so happened the lot was situated a few houses up from Lee's mother's place on Braddock Avenue. This was partly luck and partly by design. Luck in the sense that a lot was available; the design part arose from the fact that both Lee and Dorothy had grown accustomed to living on Braddock Avenue, felt at home there, especially Lee, who knew most of the families in a

Lee Collier, left, instructs a boys' church class

several block area. When, as a boy, the Collier family moved from their small farm in Georges Township, they settled at 416 Braddock. Later, the family lived at numbers 400 and 347. So the newest Braddock Avenue address would be Lee's fourth - if they ever got the house built.

There were several reasons for the delay. One was money, for despite Lee's good luck in the service and afterward, finances were tight. Witness the fact there was no family car for the longest time. In fact, an automobile didn't come the Colliers' way   until 1952, when Lee purchased from his brother a 1948 Chevrolet Fleetline that was as good as new (the Colliers wouldn't buy another car until 1964, when Lee purchased a new Buick Skylark). The second reason was lack of encouragement. Almost everyone they spoke to about the matter advised caution. Lee heard a regular litany of reasons for delay. Prices are too high, he was told. Too much risk was involved. About the only person with contrary advise was Charlie Jones, a carpenter and an old family friend who told Lee: if you can afford to build, then by all means build.

After deciding to go ahead, the Colliers got a

rude shock. Fayette Bank, where the family kept its money, turned down their loan application. Lee was dumbfounded. Called to the loan officer's home by the man's wife to repair a washing machine, Lee could not restrain himself. He said, in effect, that he would fix the machine but it was too bad the man of the house hadn't pitched in when *he* needed help.

The Colliers tried Gallatin Bank, where their GI loan application was approved. The terms were good: 4.5 percent on $14,000. With a down payment of $700, that came to $88.09 a month for 20 years.

Lee and Dorothy, not wanting to leave anything to chance, researched the kind of house they wanted. They drove to Masontown, where Jimmy Berskshire, an up-and-coming contractor, had several pre-cut houses on display. They liked what they saw but when they approached Berkshire the contractor had something else in mind. Anxious to break into the booming Uniontown housing market, Berskshire suggested a house built from scratch. He promised a sturdy ranch-style home.

The Colliers agreed, though they had some suggestions, such as placing an exhaust fan in the hallway as a means of pulling out the hot summer air, an idea they picked up at a home-show in Pittsburgh.

The house at 338 Braddock Avenue turned out to be just about perfect. Boyle Grade School and Ben Franklin Junior High School were well within walking distance for the children. A small grocery store was nearby as was the First Brethren Church. On Sunday mornings the Colliers often walked to church. They looked their best on these occasions: Dorothy and the girls in dresses, Lee and little Lee in suits and ties and starched white dress shirts.

Mr. American Legion

Paul Griffith may not have symbolized the new era that followed the war. He was, after all, a veteran of that earlier war - the war "to end all wars." He had been around for a time.

It is true he served in World War II, but it was not the type of service to make him a representative figure. He may have been the first Army reserve officer called back to duty for World War II, which was to his credit; everything else was staff work; worse, it was staff work in Washington, D.C. Major Griffith spent several years with General Lewis Hershey, head of selective service, and was later appointed assistant administrator in the Office of War Mobilization and Reconversion, in charge of retraining and reemployment. He worked there under his good friend and political mentor, Assistant Secretary of War Louis Johnson.

None of this was likely to commend him to the ex-GIs who had spent the war in the trenches fighting the enemy.

In his own way, however, Griffith came to embody the spirit of the age which emerged in the months and years immediately following the war. A thick-set man with a deep baritone voice, Griffith was elected national commander of the American Legion in the fall of 1946. The position meant plenty in those days. The Legion had helped to write and bring into being the GI Bill while the war raged. Now it would act as a spur to see that its provisions were enacted. The Legion, with over three million members, was a political dynamo, and its national commander instantly became a national figure, a political force as formidable as any major labor leader.

Griffith was 49-years-old in 1946, a graduate of Uniontown High School. His father, David, was a dairy farmer and dairy wholesaler, but the dairy business, except for a stint following World War I, appears to have been the last thing on Paul's mind. Soon after returning home (a staff sergeant with 110th Infantry, Griffith saw action in the Meuse-Argonne and was wounded near Toul,

France, where his life was saved by a French surgeon who operated without benefit to his patient of anesthesia), Griffith became a charter member of American Legion Post 51 in Uniontown and eventually post commander. Four years later, after running unsuccessfully for Congress as a Republican, he was selected state commander. In 1934, he was appointed chairman of national organizing for the Legion. From 1935 until 1940, he ran the Legion's Washington, D.C., office.

Griffith was chosen national commander at the organization's convention. The 1946 meeting in San Francisco, the first peacetime gathering since 1941, was more or less preordained to go Griffith's way. With less than a quarter of the delegates, the young turks, the World War II vets, were too few in number to challenge the Legion's old-guard. It was not likely, however, that the GI Joes of World War II could have found a more forceful advocate than Paul Griffith. He had the added benefit of possessing a fine political touch, as was evident in his first appointments to the top Legion offices: all World War II veterans.

Griffith called in his acceptance speech for more GI housing, including rental housing, and higher monthly cash outlays for job training. Afterward, he turned his attention to healing the schism between the American Legion and the government's chief of veterans affairs, General Omar Bradley, who had been appointed VA administrator by President Truman in August 1945. The dispute that erupted between Bradley (General Eisenhower's talented field commander during the war) and the American Legion originated with Griffith's predecessor, a former Republican governor of Illinois John Stelle.

Stelle accused Bradley of leading the charge against veterans' benefits and of "betraying" veterans in general. Bradley returned fire, casting Stelle in the role of the German army only more dangerous. It was "demagoguery" for anyone to promise veterans "something for nothing," Bradley asserted. (Listening to Bradley's criticism contained in a speech to Legionnaires who were at most lukewarm toward the general, Stelle said, "No one admires guts more than I do.") Days before Griffith's election, the Legion convention delegates passed a resolution which called for a congressional investigation of the VA, especially its "vast publicity staff."

The resolution was a subterfuge. The real target was Bradley, and what was at stake was power. Stelle's goal was to wrest from Bradley and the VA effective control over veterans' programs and to lodge that control with the Legion. As Charles Hurd in *The New York Times* pointed out, "supremacy" was the real issue: before Bradley's arrival at the VA, all the top leadership positions had been held by men approved by the Legion. Bradley, with five-stars on his service cap, installed his own lieutenants.

For a politician as sensitive and discerning as Griffith, the situation was especially troublesome. Nearly his whole career had been built on a deft insider's touch. It wasn't Griffith's style to openly quarrel with Bradley and the VA; he wanted to work with them. He may have sensed, too, that Stelle's efforts were a result of partisan politics and that fall's congressional campaign. Although a Republican, Griffith had no partisan ax to grind. He had worked with, through and for the Roosevelt administration in both war and peace. Above all, he could not have been unaware of President Truman's faith in Bradley and of Bradley's popularity with the nation as a whole, including Congress. Griffith met Bradley at VA headquarters in Washington. And afterward, like two heads of state, they issued a joint declaration pledging cooperation and stating their understanding that "the veteran can be helped toward a life of useful citizenship only when the government, organized veterans and the great body of the American people pull together." The two men shook hands and posed for photographs.

Practically the next thing on Griffith's agenda was a homecoming celebration in Uniontown. On November 16, 1946, upwards of 40,000 jammed his motorcade route through the city. On hand to welcome Griffith was Governor Edward Martin, the newly-chosen senator-elect from Pennsylvania, and congressman-elect Republican William Crow; both had been swept into office by a strong GOP tide in the mid-term elections.

It was a homecoming fit for a very important

person, and Griffith was that. Accompanied by his wife, the former Pearl Jennewine of Point Marion, and their children, Nancy and Paul Jr., Griffith rode in an open limousine escorted by a Legion honor guard and a 40-member drum and bugle corps. In the city's newspapers, page after page of advertisements proclaimed Griffith a great American. Ads pictured him with George Marshall. Both were hailed as "distinguished soldiers" and "famous" sons of Uniontown. Louis Johnson, who was on hand not only as Griffith's former Pentagon boss but as a former (1932) Legion national commander, turned over the organization's colors to Griffith with the words, "I give these to you now, secure in the conviction that you will carry them high and carry them unsullied." In front of a big crowd at the State Theater, Johnson, who hailed from Clarksburg, West Virginian, noted that "(Griffith) has an unusual amount of common sense. He is one commander who came up through the Legion ranks."

Griffith's father, following his son down the State Theater aisle to the stage, later told reporters, "I was just fit to bust with pride."

The hometown audience soon got a taste of where Griffith intended to lead the organization. "The American Legion," the new national commander said, "is pledged to stamping out communism wherever it rears its ugly head."

"We oppose - and and will continue to do so until the very end - communism, fascism, and any and all other devices, creeds, and tenets which have for their obvious purpose the destruction of the American system of government.

"The enemies who are boring from within are wrapping themselves in the protection of our American way of life and government. They are using our way of life as a fortress from which they can freely dispense the malignant poison of their philosophies. ... They are stirring up resentment and strife. They are seeking to divide that they may conquer."

Griffith took questions from a panel of journalists who were sitting in a studio in New York City. The live radio broadcast of *Meet The Press* late on the evening of November 16 was heard around the nation. Griffith was asked if communists should be barred from running for public office. He said he favored such a prohibition, and specifically mentioned Earl Browder, the party's top American functionary, despite Browder's recent insistence that he had left the party. The audience roared its approval when the Legion commander noted that Joseph Stalin undoubtedly still considered Browder a communist in good standing.

The next question from New York was: "Aren't veterans taking a chance of being considered in a class by themselves - a special group?" Griffith answered, "I'm one of the group that believes veterans are a special class. ... Many of the men who stayed at home set up special interest groups." He mentioned the United Mine Workers and its contentious president, John L. Lewis. "Couldn't you consider that a special interest group? They are organizing for their own behalf."

Griffith made a final mention of the GI Bill, which, he noted with only slight exaggeration, the Legion had written and enacted into law. It was "the greatest bill the world had ever seen," Griffith concluded. "Read the GI Bill and you'll see one of the most liberal pieces of legislation you have ever read."

In looking back, some of what Griffith had to say appears foolish, even mean-spirited. For instance, he saw menace in a Truman administration proposal to allow 50,000 "displaced persons" a year into the country.

These Europeans uprooted by war would undermine the government's efforts to aid veterans, Griffith argued. With well over a million former GIs drawing unemployment benefits, now was not the time to open the floodgates to the destitute of other lands. A "shocking number" of former soldiers and sailors and marines, according to Griffith, were in a state of distress - "half-housed, ill-housed or actually unhoused."

When, in May 1947, Griffith called for a one-year suspension of immigration, and told a Daughters of the American Revolution meeting in Washington that "for every legal immigrant, there were ten illegal immigrants (including seamen "jumping ship ... overseas students, foreigners arriving in transit, aliens dropping in on relatives and outlanders from the four corners of the world"), he drew a sharp rebuke from U.S. Commissioner of Immigration Earl G. Hanson. "Happily," Hanson put it, "Mr. Griffith does not speak for all veterans."

A *New York Times* editorial suggested that Griffith was inventing "bogey men" when he raised the specter of practically unlimited immigration. "A few thousand refugees cannot hurt the veteran, who is himself in countless cases a descendant of immigrant stock."

It was during this same period, following a trip to Europe, that Griffith advanced the notion to President Truman himself that the United States "bomb" the Soviet Union, or "at least somewhere over there" (meaning, presumably eastern Europe) in order to teach the communists that this country was "really in earnest and intended to protect the freedom and liberty of the people who wanted to remain free."

The President simply acknowledged Griffith's point, noting the difficult decision he had faced in dropping the atomic bomb on Japan.

December 1946: with President Truman

Hardly a foreign policy issue arose that escaped Griffith's attention. On the same day in March 1947 that Secretary of State Marshall declared at a Big Four conference in Moscow that it seemed advisable for the western allies to move toward "federalization" of the western zone in Germany, in as much as the Soviets appeared to be consolidating their grip on eastern Germany, Commander Griffith was in Cincinnati, telling Ohio Legionnaires that "we are justified in calling Russia an aggressor nation." He remarked on the "possibility" that as soon as the Soviets were strong enough, the men in the Kremlin "would make war on us." Soviet tests of guided missiles capable of traveling upwards of 3,500 miles "are not measures of peace," Griffith warned.

At a Washington press conference that summer, Griffith was asked about the crisis in Greece, where communist insurgents were undermining the Greek government. President Truman had already secured an aid package from Congress for both Greece and Turkey. The United States should do more, Griffith said, even send troops if it appeared Greece was in danger of falling into the clutches of the communists.

"The critical situation which has developed in Greece within the past few hours is a direct and dangerous head-on clash of the ideologies of democracy and communism," Griffith told reporters. "I believe that the American Legion feels that we should go all out to stop the spread of communism and Russian influence in the world." Later that day, a Legion delegation met with Undersecretary of State Robert Lovett, presumably to discuss the situation.

In the end, Griffith and the American Legion supported a foreign policy that looked and sounded remarkably like that advanced by President Truman. In addition to aid for Greece and Turkey, the Legion favored "building a dam against communism in Europe." This included support for the Marshall Plan. The 1947 Legion convention formally opposed a motion critical of the State Department, which was rapidly becoming the favorite target for right-wing Republicans angry at Truman.

As for domestic matters, Griffith called repeatedly

for Congress to lift the earnings limit that was placed on veterans who were working as they trained for new and better jobs. The Legion lobbied for the government to have some definitive plan to fight unemployment, if and when jobless numbers advanced beyond "a pre-determined dangerous limit." In a speech at Independence Hall in Philadelphia, Griffith announced the Legion would "lead the way" in support of higher salaries for public school teachers, perhaps having in mind all those millions of ex-GIs toiling away in college aiming to become teachers.

At the same time, Griffith told the Jewish War Veterans meeting in Atlantic City, "Let's get away from the foolish idea that life offers any free rides or free lunches." What he had in mind he didn't say. It could have been the Truman administration's proposal for national health insurance. "It seems almost incredible that a move has developed in the United States to deny initiative its reward. ... This is nothing but state paternalism. State paternalism is nothing but socialism."

The 1947 American Legion convention held in New

York was a riotous affair, with between 175,000 and 200,000 Legionnaires and their families in town for the occasion. The Legion parade up Fifth Avenue took most of the day, and there was hardly a pedestrian or driver in Manhattan who wasn't subject to some minor indignity during the Legion's run of the city. Water balloons were dropped from hotel windows, water pistols were squirted in faces, and traffic was halted by spur-of-the-moment "policemen" eager to clog the city's busy thoroughfares. All of this despite appeals from Griffith for Legionnaires to act their age.

Commander Griffith's plan to bring President Truman to the convention failed, owing to the President's attendance at a conference on Latin America affairs in Brazil. Through the President's close friend and military aide, Harry Vaughan, he had peppered the White House with suggestions for the presidential address. It was a long list, and included a pledge to speed construction of veterans' hospitals and an admission that in the past some presidents had been wrong and the Legion right about some issues. Griffith wanted

Truman to clarify "just what he meant in his State of the Union report to Congress last January, wherein he mentioned that except for possible minor adjustments, the Federal veterans' program was completed." He provided the President with a four-line verse "credited to a soldier of Marlborough's army ... 'God and Soldier we adore/In time of danger, not before./ The danger past and all things righted/ God is forgotten and the Soldier slighted.'" Griffith suggested Truman address the public's "shortness of memory" concerning soldierly sacrifice.

If the President of the United States could not attend the festivities, the governor of New York could and did. Thomas E. Dewey, the 1944 GOP standard-bearer, attended a large dinner hosted by Griffith at the Waldorf-Astoria Hotel. Former Minnesota governor Harold Stassen also attended. Both men later addressed the convention.

General of the Army Dwight D. Eisenhower received a thunderous ovation when he spoke to the convention. An effort to convert Eisenhower's appearance at Madison Square Garden into a demonstration of political strength for the general, who was widely considered a possible presidential candidate in 1948, was choked off by Griffith from the rostrum. As the Legionnaires from Kansas, Ike's home state, began shouting and marching the floor, he gaveled the aisles cleared. The "baffled" Kansans were quieted.

Following his stint as Legion commander, Griffith returned to Washington, to become a businessman and public relations consultant. He was called back to government service by Louis Johnson, who was named Secretary of Defense following the resignation (and eventual suicide) of the tragic James Forrestal. In September 1949, Griffith was appointed assistance secretary of defense, chiefly responsible for personnel.

Johnson's tenure at the Pentagon was rocky, to say the least. Considered tough and hard-headed coming into the post (among his other services, he had raised oodles of money for Truman's wildly successful whistle stop presidential campaign of 1948), Johnson left under a cloud, having antagonized just about the entire cabinet on account of his abrasive personality and meddling ways. Some considered him mentally unbalanced. It was said, "Truman had replaced one mental case with another." The final blow was Johnson's liaison with Senate Republicans, including GOP leader Robert Taft, and his pledge to presidential counselor Averell Harriman to secure Harriman the office of secretary of state if the two of them acted together to undermine the authority of the incumbent secretary, Dean Acheson.

Times were anxious, uncertain, unsettled. The Korean War was launched in June 1950. There was talk of communist conspirators inside the government. The Republican right-wing was on the march. The "red menace" appeared more menacing than ever.

Griffith tried to keep his head, sticking with Johnson, his "alter ego" and a Legion colleague going back to the early thirties. He didn't like how the Korea War was fought. Griffith believed that in war there was "no substitute for victory." He opposed the firing of General Douglas MacArthur from his command in Korea. He believed MacArthur was the outstanding military genius of the age. Other than these two matters and the president's sacking of Johnson, whom he said he was unimpeachable, the Republican Griffith thought Harry Truman was a "great" president.

Griffith submitted his resignation to the President in September 1950, just as Johnson did. Johnson was replaced by George Marshall. In November, as reports reached Washington that 300,000 Chinese soldiers had crossed into Korea, the White House announced acceptance of Griffith's resignation and released the text of the letter to President Truman. Becoming assistance secretary of defense had entailed "a great financial loss," Griffith wrote, and was a "burden" he felt he should not carry "any longer." He paid tribute to Johnson, and said his purpose in accepting office was to help the secretary "in the tremendous tasks before him." President Truman replied with "sincere regret," the chief executive adding, "I am happy that your loss to the government will not be final and that I may again call on you."

Griffith was never called back to public service. He died in December 1974, a resident of Chevy Chase, Maryland.

A Note on Sources & Acknowledgments

No one who writes about George C. Marshall may safely ignore the scholarship of Forrest Pogue, his biographer and oral history interviewer. Much of what is written here was based on Pogue's far-reaching work. Pogue himself was interviewed, as the text relates, in the summer of 1987. Other discussions followed on a much more informal basis. On one such occasion he related his White House conversation with President Eisenhower about Senator Joseph McCarthy and General Marshall. The Connellsville Historical Society maintains a collection of materials on the Connellsville Canteen. Two of Rose Brady's daughters, Ann and Helene, graciously consented to be interviewed as did Rita Smyth Ross, Helen Alt, Antoinette Pernatozzi Bednarek, Francis Pernatozzi Buffers, Eleanor Buttermore, Sara Kerrigan, Dorothy Keagy, Lavina Maricondi, Sally Richter, Anastasia McCarthy Smith, Louis Rulli Sorka, and Josephine Alesantrino Widmer. Gertrude Hanes and Jean J. Shields helped out with information and materials. Lisa Burger and her mother told me the story of their escape from Austria. To hear their story was a moving, vivid experience for me personally. John DePaul of Jeannette deserves a special thanks for his help with the Hilltop neighborhood story. Lee Collier, Charles Hileman, and Ed Churby were all members of the First Brethren Church . They along with John McGill sat for interviews as did Walter Radishek and the others referenced in the story who attended the Uniontown Center of Waynesburg College.

The Truman Presidential Library provided material on Paul Griffith. The Uniontown newspapers the *Morning Herald* and the *Evening Standard*, the *Connellsville Courier* and various national publications, including *The New York Times* and *Time* magazine, were invaluable. Thanks to the newsmen and newswomen who labored over the stories that helped illuminate the past in such a special way. Books consulted included *The Papers of George C. Marshall*, edited by Larry Bland; Pogue's four volumes on Marshall, especially *Education of a General, 1880-1939, Ordeal and Hope, 1939-1942* and *Organizer of Victory, 1943-1945*; *Thinking In Time by* Richard Neustadt and Ernest May; *The Glory and The Dream*, Volumes 1 and 2 by William Manchester; *The Borrowed Years, 1939-1941* by Richard M. Ketchum; *A General's Life* by Omar Bradley; *The Wise Men* by Walter Isaacson and Evan Thomas; *Truman* by David McCullough; *The Loneliest Campaign* by Irwin Ross; *Inside The Third Reich* by Albert Speer; *Our Country* by Michael Barone; *Soldier From the War Returning* by Thomas Childers; *V Was For Victory* by John Morton Blum; and *The American Heritage Picture Book of World War II*. Thanks also to the following individuals who helped in various ways through years: Larry Bland, Charles Duritsa, J.K. Folmar III, Ann Gleason Hassan, David Lester, Victoria Lionelli, the Rev. Roland Maust, Ron Nehls, Doug Robbins, Brian Shaw, Gary Thomas, and Tim Turko.

About the Author

Richard Robbins has been writing professionally since 1970, principally with the *Tribune-Review* newspapers of Pittsburgh and Greensburg, Pennsylvania. His work has appeared in *Focus Magazine, Pennsylvania Heritage Magazine, The New Castle News, The Western Pennsylvania Historical Magazine*, and *The Theodore Roosevelt Association Journal*. He is married and lives in Uniontown, Pennsylvania.

15191426R00139

Made in the USA
Charleston, SC
21 October 2012